THE LITTLE BOOK
OF
RESILIENCE

How to bounce back from adversity
and lead a fulfilling life

ROBINSON

First published in Australia in 2015 in Pan by Pan Macmillan Australia Pty Ltd.

First UK edition published in Great Britain in 2015 by Robinson

3 5 7 9 10 8 6 4 2

A CIP catalogue record for this book
is available from the British Library.

ISBN 978-1-47210-565-3 (paperback)
ISBN 978-1-47210-566-0 (ebook)

Printed and bound in Italy
Design by Matthew Johnstone

Robinson
is an imprint of
Constable & Robinson Ltd
Carmelite House
50 Victoria Embankment
London EC4Y 0DZ

An Hachette UK Company
www.hachette.co.uk

www.littlebrown.co.uk

Other bestselling books by the author

Matthew Johnstone is a passionate mental health and wellbeing advocate. He's an author, illustrator, photographer, public speaker and is also the creative director at the Black Dog Institute. He lives in Sydney with his wife and two daughters. To find out more please go to: **www.matthewjohnstone.com.au**

INNER PEACE

If you can start the day without coffee,

If you can always be cheerful, ignoring aches and pains,

If you can resist complaining and boring people with your troubles,

If you understand when your loved ones are too busy to give you any time,

If you can take criticism and blame without resentment,

If you can conquer tension without drugs,

If you can relax without alcohol,

If you can sleep without sleeping pills …

Well then, you're probably the family dog.

ANON

THE LITTLE BOOK OF
RESILIENCE

re·sil·ience
noun
1.
the power or ability to return to the
original form, position, etc., after being
bent, compressed, or stretched; elasticity.
2.
ability to recover readily from illness,
depression, adversity, or the like; buoyancy.

Written and Illustrated by
Matthew Johnstone

ROBINSON

FOR MY WONDERFUL FAMILY
(BOTH IMMEDIATE AND EXTENDED)

My heartfelt thanks to Alex Craig,
Libby Turner and the staff at
Pan Macmillan Australia for believing in what I do.
To Pippa Masson and the staff at Curtis Brown
for their support, advice and guidance.
To the Black Dog Institute for the incredible work they do,
and being a continual source of inspiration and support.
And to everyone I've road-tested this book on,
thank you for your time and your valued feedback.
To lostandtaken.com, thank you for the textures once again.

Foreword

Watch any current affairs show on any given day and you're bound to see someone who has come out the other side of some bizarre, horrific, near-fatal, life-challenging event. For those affected, it's often a life-defining crossroad where everything changes, where they take stock of their lives and question what is truly important and alter their lives accordingly.

I feel I've had a pretty blessed life but along the way there have been a few defining moments.
I had a near-death experience following a massive asthma attack.
A friend and I were assaulted; he had his front teeth knocked out and I was chased by a guy with a knife who said he was going to kill me.
I stood a block from the World Trade Center when it came down.
And sporadically throughout my adult life, I have battled and thankfully overcome depression.
All these events were horrible, painful and frightening but in many ways they forged the person, the father, husband and friend that I am today. I wouldn't want to repeat any of the above but I wouldn't change anything either, mostly because I can't. Collectively, they opened my eyes to what I hold dear and value in my life.

Viktor Frankl, who miraculously survived three years in Nazi concentration camps including Auschwitz, wrote in his book *Man's Search for Meaning* that while we may have little control over events in our lives, what we have paramount control over is how we respond.

In many ways that's what this book is all about. We all have a story. We all have a journey, with both good and bad. We all have the ability to overcome difficulty and grow from the experience.

Whatever is going on in your life at this moment, I truly hope this little book gives some inspiration, comfort, guidance and smiles. I also hope this finds you well wherever you may be.

Matthew Johnstone

PART I

To the uninitiated, resilience could be the secret ingredient in a fancy age-defying face cream.

In fact, resilience is all about developing a degree of flexibility and acceptance when it comes to life events.

It's not so much about what happens to you at the time of the event but how you respond or bounce back afterward.

Our lives, experiences, upbringings and families are all different, but it would be fair to say that most of us set out quietly hoping, and secretly expecting, to live a happy, successful and healthy life. This life would ideally be topped with some meaning and purpose, with a generous side order of solid and sustaining relationships.

BUT LIFE
DOESN'T ALWAYS
GO TO PLAN
OR PLAY FAIR.

This doesn't mean we should live with a sense of endless foreboding. It's an opportunity to live and experience each day

FULLY

One of the few sureties of life is that nothing is certain.

Peppered through our day-to-day continuum will
be curve balls, surprises and blindsides.
Not all of them are good, not all of them are bad.

These are the HILLS AND DALES OF LIFE.

SOME HILLS AND DALES OF LIFE

Love & Heartbreak

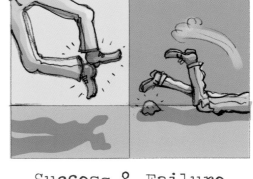

Success & Failure

Excitement & Boredom

Dreams & Realities

Health & Illness

Happiness & Sadness

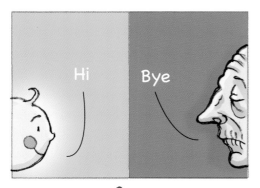

Life & Death

If we can learn to accept early on that life is going to be a mixed bag of positive and negative experiences, we're going to be much better equipped to deal with whatever life will inevitably throw at us down the track.

Another surety in life
is you cannot change the past.

You cannot change something
that may have happened to you.

You cannot change what someone
may have done to you.

You cannot change what you
may have done to others.

You cannot change your family,
as much as you might like to sometimes.

But with a degree of acceptance, understanding and insight, and the right help, we can alter perceptions, beliefs and outcomes of the less desirable events in our lives

FOR THE BETTER.

Accepting what we can and cannot change is one of the most important aspects of understanding resilience.

It's learning to work with and grow what's right in our lives while accepting, but not putting all our energy into, what's not.

Just because we stop physically growing doesn't mean we should stop growing intellectually, emotionally and spiritually.

Obviously you can change your weight, your hair colour, your wrinkles or the whiteness of your teeth but it's more of a challenge to change what lies behind the eyes.

When it comes to a lifetime of learned habits, rigid beliefs and the scar of life-altering events, we can always *evolve,*

knead,

enhance,

engage

and

improve.

egative events can be terrible and painful.

They can be life-changing and soul-destroying, both at the time and for some time after.

Yet nowhere does it state that the net effect should stain the rest of our lives, like a blighted tattoo.

Quite often the things we deem terrible can emerge as lateral teachers. The catch is that this wisdom can only be gleaned if we're prepared to learn and grow from the experience.

It's not that we should forget, it's just many choose not to learn or reflect on such events and thus become stuck in their own situation.

It's important to stress that resilience isn't necessarily gained only from going through something unfortunate. We can create strength and mental fortitude by going through tough positive experiences: climbing a mountain, completing a degree, having a child, running a marathon and so forth.

Tough doesn't always mean terrible, painful or tragic.

We humans are highly averse to pain, be it mental, emotional or physical.

We'll go over it, under it, around it or away from it – rarely do we intentionally go through it.

It sounds unfair but to truly get over something, you need to go through it.

When we fully embrace and try to understand
the situation and embark on a gentle and considered way
forward, we can come out the other side stronger for it.

We can become kinder, wiser, more understanding,
more compassionate and we can live with
a greater sense of purpose and meaning.

Humans are the consummate performers. We each invest vast amounts of energy into our 'show face'. This is the face we present to the world, the face we want others to see and to believe in. We could run power stations with the amount of energy we invest in our show faces.

Why do we do this? Is it shame, stigma, ego, not wanting to complain, not wanting to appear weak, not wanting to be a burden?

If we took half the energy that we invest into covering something up and used it to actually understand and heal the wound, we could move through it and get on with life a lot quicker.

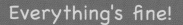

When it comes to being authentic, vulnerable and speaking from the heart, we have to look beyond the perceived dangers of doing so.

Our history, fears, thoughts and distorted beliefs can hold us hostage in our own minds. We have to be brave and focus on the freedom of being our true selves.

At some stage, there has to be a sort of surrender to the process, the situation and the outcome. If we are talking to the right people, getting the right help, and doing the things that bring wellbeing into our lives

then that is all we can do.

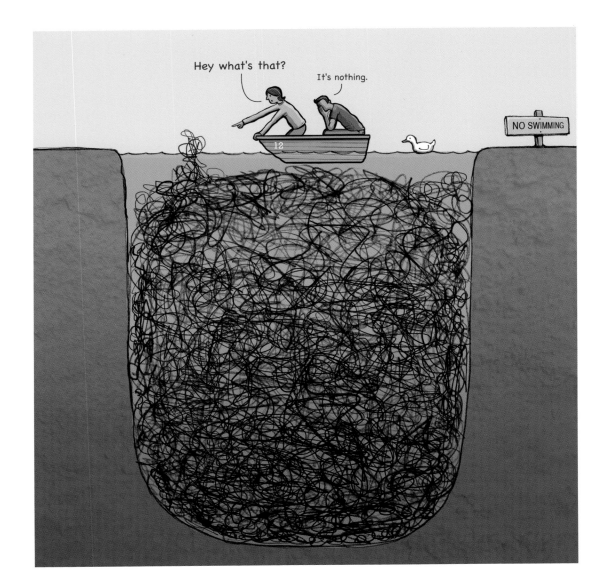

When faced with any kind of adversity in life, we often look for the quick fix, the get-out-of-jail-free card, and when that's not forthcoming, we will swallow the problem into the vast lake of our being, hoping to suppress its shock and awe.

This lake has immense capacity. We can keep turning up with our toxic swill and dumping it in there for a long time.

The problem is that the lake has a bottom and if we're not processing, recycling and mopping up, the quagmire will overflow. This can not only affect us mentally and physically but can also impact those around us.

WHERE TO FROM HERE?

Do we stay down or get up?

Do we remain a victim or become a survivor?

Are we weakened or strengthened?

Do we stay stuck or do we move forward?

Can we make a negative situation a turning point for change?

Others can and will help along the way but in the end it's really all up to you.

The first step is to acknowledge that there is a problem:

- I am not coping.
- I have a mental health issue.
- I have a physical impairment.
- I have a substance addiction.
- I have been abused.
- I am anxious.
- I find no joy in anything ...

It requires total honesty with yourself and then with others.

Although the first step of recovery or seeking help can be the biggest and most daunting, it is also the most important.

There will inevitably be many steps and stumbles that follow but from this moment on, with the right amount of determination, perseverance and help, it's a matter of continually moving forward and upward, one step at a time.

I OWN

MY

PROBLEMS.

MY PROBLEMS DON'T OWN ME.

A vitally important virtue is patience. In this world of everything being instant, we expect the same when it comes to our difficulties.

The secret is to take the problem and break it down into manageable chunks.

During this mining process, there are gems to be found.

These gems can be love and support we didn't realise we had. An inner strength we never knew existed. A new and improved way of expressing ourselves. There can be valuable insights and understandings about ourselves and others.

It seems counterintuitive but there is real strength to be found in learning how to be vulnerable, authentic and to speak from a place of truth.

This can prove challenging because we've had a lifetime of building up our show face, our defences, sleight of hand and visual illusions.

When we speak from the heart and learn to be genuine, there is no shadow in which we can hide. There is freedom in this and when we share, we allow others to do the same.

Those important people in our lives will generally respond favourably to emotional honesty and will help as best they can.

If they don't, perhaps it's because it hits too close to the bone of their own experiences, shortcomings or fears.

Another vitally important aspect of resilience is developing a sense of compassion for yourself and what you've been through.

Self-compassion isn't being self-indulgent or soft. It's not about feeling sorry for yourself, it's about <u>not</u> beating yourself up for feeling bad, feeling pain or not coping.

No one persecutes us mentally and emotionally more than ourselves.

Self-compassion is about being gentle and kind with yourself as you would an infant, the elderly or someone you love. It's also about doing good things for yourself like exercise, meditation, eating well and helping others.

When we become compassionate to our own needs, it's only natural that we then become compassionate and empathetic to others, which is always a good thing.

It is perfectly

K...

... not to feel

K

The trick is not getting stuck.

When it comes to the way that we think of ourselves and what may currently be going on in our lives, it's very important to discern fact from fiction. Our thoughts are phenomenally powerful. They can become intrusive, repetitive, obsessive and very persuasive.

The movies we play in our minds can be IMAX in size, with Dolby surround sound, 3D and impressive production values.
These movies are often horror films, screening in the small hours of the morning.

Yet as real and convincing as these movies can be, you have to remind yourself that ...

... THOUGHTS *are* **NOT**

FACTS

Take a moment to consider what this means and then tattoo it onto your brain.

Browse any self-help section in a book store and you'll find plenty of books with an emphasis on having happy thoughts, positive mantras and creating lovely manifestations.

There's nothing intrinsically wrong with this but rather than avoiding unpleasant thoughts, feelings and fears, why not try embracing them? Why not try and understand why you're having them in the first place?

Don't sweep them under the rug, don't suppress them, don't drown them with alcohol and other forms of self-medication.

Take them on, challenge them at their own game.

Say 'do your worst!' because by this stage, they probably have.
If they are thoughts that frighten you, then turn them into something
worthy of a cartoon, make them comical. Change the story and you can
change the outcome.

If you really don't feel in control of your thoughts or feelings, talk to
a mental health professional.

FEARless

One of the ways we can address our worrying thoughts and fears is to make room for some 'worry time'. Allow five to ten minutes every other day, writing down everything you deem frown-inducing.

When the list is complete, take a moment to quietly read it through then take small pleasure with some ceremony in destroying what you've written. Screw it up, rip it up, stamp on it or pop it on the BBQ.

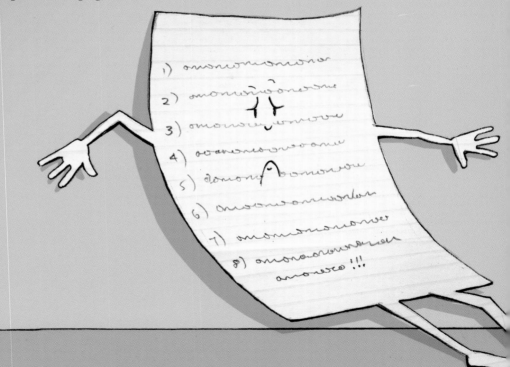

Once done, literally leave your worries behind and get on with your day, knowing that you've drawn a mental line in the sand.

This exercise is not intended to solve all your problems; however the very process of acknowledging your issues is highly cathartic and allows more space for positive solutions.

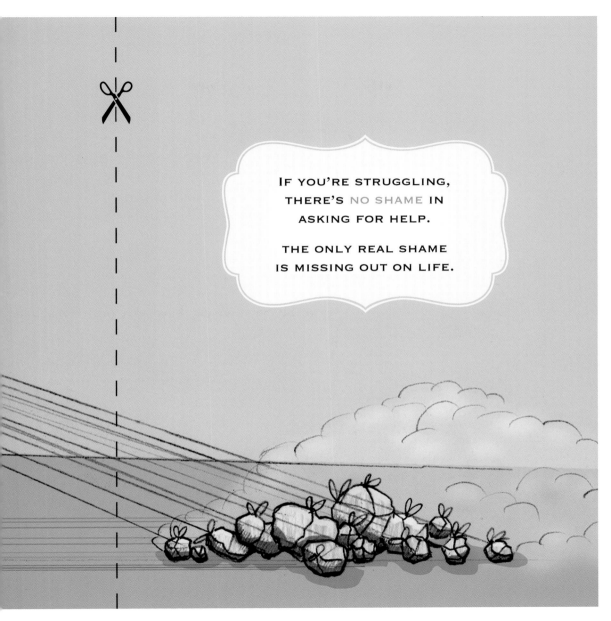

IF YOU'RE STRUGGLING,
THERE'S NO SHAME IN
ASKING FOR HELP.

THE ONLY REAL SHAME
IS MISSING OUT ON LIFE.

Having a shoulder to cry on can be helpful, but if you're not coping emotionally or mentally, or you're facing a more serious life event, that person may not be well-equipped or qualified to deal with the issue at hand. Which is why it can be worthwhile talking to a complete stranger in the form of a psychiatrist, a psychologist or a counsellor; they are all trained to help when we're under mental duress.

They can help us reframe the way we think. They can change the way we perceive a problem. They can help us challenge negative beliefs and can give us useful cognitive tools to help manage most situations and feelings.

It can be beneficial to educate yourself about the different roles in mental health and to understand different styles of treatment and therapy. In doing so, it won't feel like such a mystery and will give you a greater sense of control over your situation.

When considering a mental health professional, think of it like shopping for a good pair of shoes; it should feel like the right fit. If you're going to tell a stranger your problems, you should feel like you're in a place of sanctuary.

They are not there to be your friend, they are not there to judge, to criticise or make you do things you don't want to do.

It's a professional relationship where empathy, support and understanding combined with a solid plan toward recovery and wellbeing should all make for a positive outcome.

How to Build, Develop and Nurture Resilience

A lot of what you're about to read will seem obvious or even perhaps a bit twee, but all the things that help to build resilience and wellbeing are those that we constantly neglect to do for ourselves.
To live a mentally and physically robust life is all about 'life management' and the discipline to do the things that make us feel good and give us strength.

Often you hear *'I don't have time to exercise, to meditate, to eat well'*. The net result of this attitude is that people only stop when they're too sick to carry on. So make time. Do it for yourself. Do it for others.
Prevention is, after all, the greatest cure.

PART II

It has been clinically proven that regular exercise is as effective for treating mild to moderate depression and anxiety as antidepressants.

Exercise can make a profound difference on our outlook. It boosts our mood, it helps us to lose weight, it can fight myriad diseases and it can also improve our sleep.

Around 30 minutes of physical activity daily is recommended.

This does not mean that we have to run marathons, swim oceans or live at the gym. We can have have our regular exercise like walking, running, swimming etc. interspersed with incidental activities such as getting off the bus a couple of stops early, taking the stairs instead of the lift, walking to get (a healthy) lunch instead of sitting at our desks, or treating housework as a workout.

Sweat out the bad stuff so you can experience more of the good.

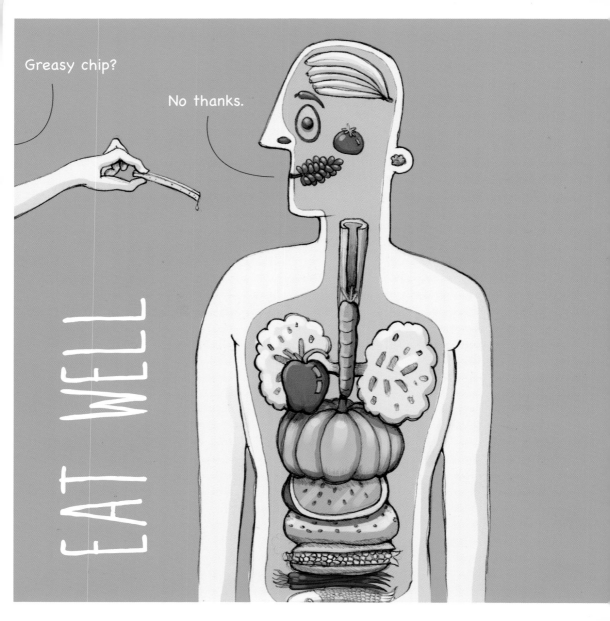

Quite often we eat in accordance with how we're feeling. We tend to eat badly when we're stressed, bored, lonely or even celebrating. This 'comfort food' can make us feel like rubbish.

If you want to know just how well you can feel, try going on a detox for four to six weeks. Don't be surprised if you feel a bit lousy in the beginning; your body will be howling for what it craves. There may be headaches and feelings of agitation but they should pass in the first week or so. After that you'll start to feel more energised, focused, motivated, happy and you'll begin to look better too.

By removing the usual suspects of caffeine, sugar, red meat, alcohol, wheat and dairy, you'll be nudged toward a diet of fruit, vegetables, whole grains, fish, chicken and dairy alternatives.

Don't think of it as a 'diet', but as the ultimate self-compassionate experiment that will do you a world of good. Your palate will simplify to appreciate more delicate and subtle flavours. You'll realise how much of society is based around passive addictions and habitual behaviour.

How often do you hear, I can't do without *'my morning coffee'*, *'my glass of wine with dinner'*, *'my evening choccy'*? Just remove that little word *'can't'* from your vocabulary and realise you *'can'* do without these foods.

Once you discover how well you can feel, you will gravitate toward a fresh and natural diet that will hopefully become *'most of the time'* rather than *'some of the time'*.

Put some time into researching the best approach for you, and drink lots of water while you're at it.

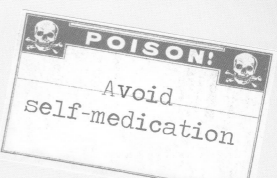
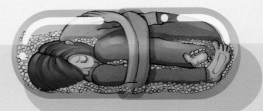

Cocaine can give us confidence.
Ecstasy can make us lovey-dovey.
Marijuana can chill us out.
Alcohol helps us to relax and socialise.

These, and the other potential effects of drugs and alcohol, can be quite enticing to anyone who is stressed, depressed, anxious, bored, feeling peer pressure or has a desire to experiment. They can all deliver on their promises but at a cost; often a big cost.

It's the cost of damage inflicted on the brain and the long-term effect on mental health. It's the cost of addiction and the overall cost in treatment and loss of productivity to society.

Alcohol, the most publicly condoned of the lot, is responsible for the lion's share of assaults, hospitalisations, DUIs and vandalism, and many health problems.

The biggest reason people abuse drugs or drink alcohol to excess is that they see them as the panacea to their problems – they blunt, diffuse or suspend pain and reality. In the end, this solution can become the biggest problem of all.

Do yourself, your brain and society a massive favour by getting more out of life, not more 'out of it'.

When good sleep goes, so does everything that depends on it; your mood, your memory, your ability to get things done and to focus, and it makes you feel generally lousy. Having rubbish sleep is like pouring alcohol on your cornflakes: it's just not a good way to start the day.

Bad sleep not only affects us cognitively but if we continually have bad sleep, it can increase obesity, heart disease and diabetes – and it can shorten your life expectancy.

People need different amounts of sleep but the golden rule is around seven to eight hours of decent sleep per night to function properly.

Invest in a really good bed and bedding; you spend over a third of your life there. Try to avoid caffeine, alcohol, exercise, stimulating movies or video games right before bed. Have a bath. Have a warm drink. Read a book. Dim the lights. Listen to relaxing music. Write lists of concerns prior to sleep. Learn deep breathing relaxation techniques.

MAKE YOUR BED A SACRED PLACE.

Most of us breathe incorrectly. Our breathing is wonderfully automated, so we don't give it much thought but perhaps we should. Most of us breathe as if our lungs end just below our collarbones: short, shallow, quick breaths that nourish very little.

In simple terms, if oxygen is life, we're not getting the most out of it.

Breathing deeply increases our energy, creates better mental clarity and helps our organs and blood to detox.

To see how we should breathe, look to a baby. They breathe naturally and deeply, into their stomachs while expanding their rib cage.

The next time you feel stressed or angry, remove yourself from the situation, find a quiet place and take five to ten slow deep breaths right down to your navel. Put your hand on your stomach and make it rise.
Breathe in fully for four beats, hold for two beats, then exhale slowly until your lungs feel empty. Repeat until you feel calm and nourished.

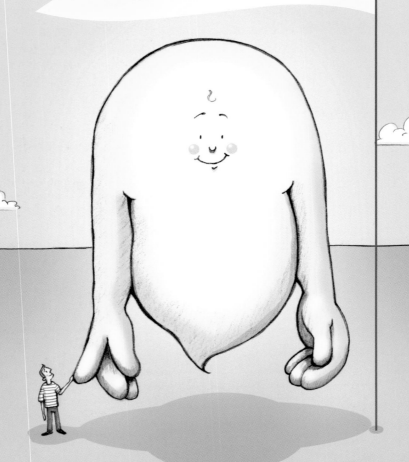

It could be said that social media is amplifying society's level of narcissism. There is a lot more *'I'* and *'me'*, less *'you'*, *'us'* and *'we'*. This 'selfie culture' can also lead to a sense of isolation, which is another good reason to make life less about you and more about others.

Connect to something bigger than yourself. It could be your faith, your family, your job, your community, the environment, a cause, a sports team and so forth.

When we give of ourselves, life gives back. We feel fulfilled, connected and have a greater sense of purpose.

Do and believe in things that make you glow, that bring you joy, that feel effortless.

It's easy to say *'who am I in this world of billions?'* but everyone has their role to play, everyone has something they can offer, everyone can be of service, everyone can create positive change.

Trying something new can push us out of our comfort zones, which in many ways is the very reason to do it. Attempting new things can be daunting but they can get us off our butts, open us up to new experiences, new skills, new ways of thinking and people with similar interests.

We can discover facets of ourselves that we never knew existed. It's also a wonderful way to connect with the greater community and to feel a part of something. Not only can this be fun but it can bring fulfilment and a new-found enthusiasm for life.

So challenge yourself by joining a club, a group, a community project, a support group or volunteer for something you're passionate about.

Apparently those who learn another language are less likely to develop dementia. So trying something *nouveau* clearly has major mental health benefits too.

To evolve, get involved.

HAVE A DIGITAL DETOX

ONLINE

OFFLINE

Computers, tablets and smartphones are wonderful examples of human ingenuity, endeavour and achievement.

Useful, smart and, at times, indispensable but next time you're waiting for a plane, train or bus, do a quick tally of how many people are on devices.

Emails, texts, social media and gaming all keep us from what's going on around us and connecting with one another. It's an addictive form of stimulation and diversion.

It seems we are losing our ability to sit, to observe, to daydream, to converse, to be bored. When the brain is constantly kept busy by bright shiny things, it becomes increasingly difficult to quieten it down.

Modern-day self-esteem comes externally from how many 'friends' we have or how many 'likes' and 'retweets' we acquire.

Playdates have become kids leaning over tablets or gaming devices.

Smartphones have become uninvited guests at dinner tables.

Workplaces have become quieter because it's easier to type than it is to walk and talk.

Technology is by no means bad, but sometimes to tune in to life, we need to 'turn off' more often.

ff

Music is the season for our moods. It is the dog-eared bookmark of our lives.
It is a force that motivates us to tap, hum, sing and dance.
It can make the hairs on the backs of our necks stand in ovation.
It is something that connects us all on a tribal and heartfelt level.

Music is the most wonderful, intangible human endeavour that has no reason
for being other than to bring a sense of:

Joy   Calm   Sorrow

INSPIRATION

Rele^ase   Relaxation

Bliss   REFLECTION

ENERGY   ... and so forth

See some, play some, listen to some.

Keep GOOD Company

As you get older you begin to realise that life is short. Get the most out of it by being around people who make you feel good while making a conscious and deliberate effort to extricate yourself from those who are toxic, make you feel bad or enable you in activities that are not good for you.

A person of positive influence should be a good listener, be interested in you and your life (as you should be for them). They should be supportive of you and never put you down. Someone you share values with, can laugh with, and where conversations flow naturally.

People who are cynical, sarcastic, destructive or full of contempt bring no added value and simply drain what is good out of life, namely yours.

Deep down we all know what sort of person we are and how we behave around others. If you tilt toward the negative side of the scales, it's never too late to change, to get help and improve this aspect of yourself. When you hurt others you hurt yourself. So start by becoming your own best friend and go from there.

Learn Forgiveness

If someone has done the wrong thing by you, one of the best (and sometimes toughest) things you can do is find a place in your heart for forgiveness. When you forgive you can let go; when you let go, you can move forward.

This by no means condones what they have done.
You don't have to see them again. You don't even have to tell them.

Forgiveness simply allows you to get on with your life.

You can tell your story over and over, and you'll probably get the same validating *'how terrible!'* response, but in the end anger, resentment and contempt all have a terribly corrosive effect on the soul.

As you ponder forgiveness, consider what may have happened in that person's life that made them who they are and how it may have forged what they did.

If it is you that has done the wrong thing, forgive yourself; we are more than the sum total of our mistakes. Learn from the mistake and do the right thing and make amends for your actions. It is never too late.

Never understimate the power of a meaningful apology, nor the power of being able to accept one.

Do the Stuff You Love

Why do avid gardeners passionately do what they do?

They are outside, they receive vitamin D from the sun. It's physical work, there's a connection to the earth. There's great planning, forecasting and working with the seasons. Then there's a return on time and labour invested in the way of a beautiful garden that provides flowers, fruits or vegetables. These gifts not only feed, but can bring a real sense of joy, pride and achievement.

If you don't think you have an activity in your life that brings you these sorts of benefits, think back to an activity you did as a child that could make time stand still. Where the effort for this pastime was akin to riding a bike with the wind behind your back. There were no thoughts of yesterday or tomorrow, just a laser-beam intensity directed to the project at hand. We might call this bliss, a halcyon bubble or our happy place.

If you haven't integrated an aspect, or an interpretation of this activity into your adult life, ask yourself: why not?

Make a time in your day, week or month that is all about you and the thing that makes your heart sing and your mind smile.

It can be the difference between doing life and living it.

Sitting in silence or becoming more observant of the current moment tends to be one of the more challenging wellbeing activities. It goes against the very nature of our overly active and increasingly stimulated brains.

There are myriad mental and physical benefits to learning meditation and mindfulness. To start with, it opens up more space for creativity and productivity while instilling a quiet calm that can weather any storm. We are also more engaged with what we're doing and who we're with.

It's not about having <u>no</u> thoughts, it's more about not engaging with, reacting to or chasing them. It's about quietly observing, without judgement.
It's about quietening your mind, one breath at a time.

People often say *'I tried meditation once and I just couldn't do it!'* It's a bit like saying *'I went for a run once and when I came back I wasn't fit!'*. Just like exercise and eating well, it's so worth pursuing.

BIG THANKS

FOR LITTLE THINGS

Rather than focussing on everything that is wrong or missing in your life, try looking at what is right, then practise thinking and saying *thanks for that*.

We shouldn't hold out on our gratitude for the bigger house, the fancier car, the pay rise; it should be for the unexpected hug, cup of tea, hanging out with a good friend, a fine day, an unexpected compliment, a drawing by a child and so forth.

Think of yourself as an 'Appreciation Collector', the more you collect, the bigger the collection; the bigger the collection, the greater the value we find in life. It all adds up.

Gratitude is simply the palette that paints a better picture of life.

Dame Grace Manyblessings

Sir Gracias Thanksalot

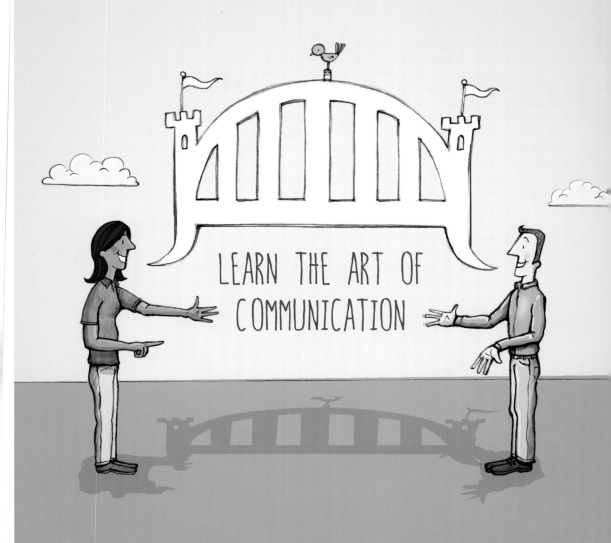

The majority of us are capable of listening and talking but ask yourself, do you do both of these activities well?

Being a great communicator is a skill worth learning.

There's an art to being able to listen to where someone is coming from without instantly going on the defensive, without having to constantly jump in or 'one-up' with a story of your own or refraining from the need to tell them what they should do. Being contemplative, considered and thoughtful in any form of conversation is a form of personal mastery. As is being able to clearly articulate what you may be going through.

There's nothing worse than being talked at or not being listened to.

Just as there's nothing greater than thinking *we could have talked all night*.

SET YOURSELF A GOAL

If you have a degree of discontent or feel stuck about how your life is panning out, having a goal is a good way to change the current trajectory.

Goals help bring out your true potential. They create energy, focus and they force you to live your life more consciously.

Everyone has a dream, a novel, an invention, a movie idea and so often these are realised by others because they 'did' rather than pondered.

Often we begin to hatch a plan and then think of a million reasons why it couldn't happen in the same thought bubble.

So ask yourself, if time and money were no object what would you love to do?

The answer could be a massive hairy, scary, bodacious idea or could be something relatively simple. Whether it's 10 steps or 1000 steps to that goal, take that first step. Make a pledge with yourself that each day, each week, each month, you will do something small, medium and large toward your goal. You have nothing to lose but the time you spend doing something that doesn't fulfil you.

Talk to people, get advice, find a mentor, be passionate.

If it doesn't work out, you will have extended yourself, learnt new skills, met new people and perhaps discovered other ideas worth exploring.

If it does work out, the first question you'll ask is *why didn't I do this sooner?*.

REWARD
THYSELF

When major birthdays roll around we often find ourselves asking where did all the time go? Busy work, family and social schedules tend to make time fly and it only seems to go faster as we get older.

So step on the brakes every once in a while and take a tally of all the things you've done that have made you and possibly others proud. Recognise and honour your path, your progress and take pride in what you've achieved, both big and small.

It could be overcoming a difficulty, it could be your kids, your garden, a project at work, a ship made out of tooth picks.

Whatever it is, visualise a squadron of jets flying overhead, spurred on by a huge brass band and a spectacular fireworks display while graciously saying *'I did that!'*.

No matter what adverse life experience you've
been through, there is incredible catharsis to be found in
the telling of your story and what you've learnt from it.

Joining a support group, volunteering for a cause,
writing a book or a blog lets people who are maybe
going through something similar know that they are
not alone, flawed, failed or doomed.

When you give of yourself, life gives back.

*Help yourself by
helping others.*

Final Thoughts

Appreciate little things.

Nurture compassion.

Find joy in the moment.

Learn to quiet your mind.

Strive for wellbeing.

Speak from the heart.

Grow from adversity.

Always hold onto hope.

Live with love.

END ON AN UP

There are an incredible number of inspiring people who have overcome amazing odds. Here are just a few for you to google should you need some inspiration.

Bethany Hamilton

Douglas Bader

Kris Carr

Helen Keller

Viktor Frankl

Mark Zupan

Malala Yousafzai

Nick Vujicic

Candace Lightner

Turia Pitt

Stephen Hawking

Bruce & Denise Morcombe

RESOURCES*

MENTAL HEALTH
www.blackdoginstitute.org.au
www.overcoming.co.uk
www.mentalhealth.org.uk
www.mind.org.uk
www.sane.org.uk
www.samaritans.org
www.patient.co.uk
www.depressionalliance.org
www.adviceguide.org.uk
www.rethink.org
www.papyrus-uk.org (teen)
www.mindfull.org (teen)
www.youngminds.org.uk (teen)
www.youthspace.me (teen)

BETTER SLEEP
www.sleepcouncil.org.uk
www.sleepio.com

FOOD / NUTRITION
www.nutrition.org.uk

RELATIONSHIPS
www.relate.org.uk

DRUGS AND ALCOHOL
www.alcoholics-anonymous.org.uk
www.na.org
www.alcoholconcern.org.uk
www.adfam.org.uk
www.talktofrank.com

MEDITATION AND MINDFULNESS
www.actmindfully.com.au
www.compassionatemind.co.uk
www.compassionatewellbeing.com
www.self-compassion.org
www.mindfulselfcompassion.org
www.wildmind.org

PHYSICAL HEALTH & EXERCISE
www.nhs.uk
7 minute workout (app)
Couch to 5K (running app)
Zombies, Run! (running app)

GET INVOLVED
www.health.org.uk
www.charitychoice.co.uk

*There are so many wonderful (mostly free) resources out there, this is just the tip of the iceberg.

NOTES

NOTES

NOTES

And lo and behold, there's a text there from the exact bookworm I'd just been thinking about. Leaning forward, I read the message.

What's the dress code for tomorrow?

Smiling, I nab the phone—hot blonde forgotten. My fingers race across the screen.

Summer casual. Flirty if you're feeling it.

I had texted her the address of the wedding last night, which is Erik and Blue's house. I'd told her there would be valet parking, and I'd meet her in front at the valet stand at 5:45 PM.

She had simply replied, *Okay.*

That had flummoxed me.

The woman didn't show a single bit of curiosity in the man she'd agreed to go out with, to a wedding of all things. Disappointingly, that told me she wasn't the slightest bit interested in me. Instead, she was just fulfilling her obligation to attend the weddings with me.

I'm heartened by the fact she's reaching out now, because, truth be told, she could have figured out what to wear to a wedding on her own.

I wait for her to reply, but nothing comes back.

"So, my name's Heather," the blonde says, touching my arm. I'm startled, having completely forgotten about her.

My head snaps up, first to take in the gorgeous creature in front of me, who bats her eyelashes. Then around the table to find all four of my buds snickering at my uncharacteristic lack of game.

I look past her to Baden. "Hey man… will you get her a drink? I'll be just a moment."

"Yeah, sure," Baden replies with an easygoing smile. The blonde knows she's just been dismissed by me as a potential hookup, so she turns her charms to Baden, looping her arm over his shoulder and leaning into him.

By the time I turn back to my phone, she's forgotten completely. I send Clarke another text.

Or… you don't have to go with flirty if you're not feeling it. You're not feeling it, are you?

I stare at my phone. In the back of my mind, I vaguely wonder what the hell is wrong with me. I just turned down a guaranteed fuck tonight so I could poke at the fascinating bookstore owner who doesn't seem to want much to do with me.

I'm so surprised when she responds I nearly drop my phone.

It's hard to be flirty via text. Also, I suck at flirting.

I bark out a laugh. Lifting my eyes to see Jim and Jett watching me curiously, I drop my gaze back down to the phone.

Believe it or not, it's kind of attractive you acknowledge that.

It takes her a few moments to respond, which makes it clear the conversation is most likely over.

Goodnight, Professor. See you tomorrow.

I can't let that go, so I type back.

Professor?

Her reply is nearly instant, because she was expecting me to ask.

Yeah… professor, because you totally schooled me in classic literature yesterday.

My heart actually skips a beat when she adds on a crying-laughing emoji.

Which means she finds me at least partially funny, and that's something.

In this moment, one thing becomes abundantly clear via this exchange. There isn't going to be any hookup tomorrow night after the wedding and reception. That's not her game, nor her style.

And oddly… I'm okay with that.

CHAPTER 4

Clarke

F OR THE FIRST time ever, I doubt my GPS as it guides me into a neighborhood filled with gargantuan-sized houses. Aaron had told me there would be valet parking, so I just assumed the wedding would be at some type of public venue. At the very least, at this neighborhood's clubhouse, yet the map leads me right to a salmon-colored Mediterranean-styled home that has to be at least seven- to-eight-thousand-square feet if it's an inch.

Sure enough, there's a valet stand in front with five tuxedoed men waiting to take cars and park them down the street so people don't have to.

I pull my little Honda Civic hatchback manufactured circa 2009 directly behind what looks to be a Ferrari. Making sure to leave plenty of room between our cars, I then step out, immediately assisted by one of the valets. Scrambling inside my little clutch purse, I curse when I realize I don't have anything smaller than a ten. I hand it to him and move to the curb, giving a last glance at my little car. It's been so trusty and loyal, and I love it far more than any Ferrari.

"That dress is definitely flirty," a deep voice behind me says. I whirl to find Aaron Wylde standing exactly where he said he'd wait, holding the gift he'd bought from me two days ago.

Damn it… I have to admit he looks exceedingly handsome in a pair of light gray slacks and a lavender-colored dress shirt. It's hot as hell—love a summer day in Phoenix—and I'm guessing that's why he's without the matching jacket. His blond hair is swept back in waves from his face and whereas he was sporting some stubble when I met him the other day in my store, he's clean-shaven now.

I'd chosen a sleeveless dress in a light coral that complements the vivid coloring of my hair. It's made of chiffon, and it swishes lazily around my knees when I walk.

And when I say I'd chosen, I mean I raided Veronica's closet as I had not one single thing suitable for a wedding. Luckily, Veronica has more than enough to compensate. It was just as convenient to raid her closet as to go shopping.

Cheaper, too.

I step onto the sidewalk, then move toward Aaron.

Other cars pull up, people spill out, then start heading toward the front door of the sprawling mansion.

Aaron's eyes rake over me, making me feel entirely self-conscious and just a bit pretty when I see the approval on his face. "You look beautiful," he says, turning to offer his arm.

"Thank you," I reply demurely, trying to remember the last time a man said that. Searching my memory, I work backward in time through the men I've dated in the past and I have to go all the way back to "him" before I can remember such a compliment.

I immediately scrub "him" from my mind, not wanting to taste the bile in the back of my throat, which is a frequent occurrence with those memories.

"You clean up very well yourself, Professor," I tell Aaron, which is a phenomenal understatement.

He laughs as we walk up to the house. "I love that. Professor."

"You really did school me," I mutter, still a bit put out I'd gotten taken so easily. There's a bit of a line waiting to get in the door, so I take the time to say, "You didn't tell me that your friend who was getting married was rich as sin. I might have suggested a nicer gift than a wine opener."

Aaron laughs again. It's that sort of effortless sound a person makes when they find genuine humor in life. "Trust me... Erik and Blue might be rich, but they are very down to earth. In fact, beer bottle opener would have been more appropriate."

"All evidence to the contrary," I say, sweeping my hand against the backdrop of the grand house as we move onto the porch.

Standing inside the doorway, I'm surprised to find a boy—no, a *man*—in a wheelchair with another tall man standing beside him. It appears they are the welcoming committee.

Aaron pulls his arm loose from my hand and holds his fist out to the man in the wheelchair. "Hey, Billy... big day, huh?"

Billy smiles broadly, sort of rocking back and forth before bringing his own fist up to bump against Aaron's. He doesn't say anything, and I guess he might be non-verbal.

Aaron introduces me. "Billy... this is my friend, Clarke." Turning, he says, "This is Blue's brother, Billy."

I bend slightly, bringing my face more in line with his so he doesn't have to look up. I'm not sure what to say, but I say what anyone might to the young man. "Hi, Billy... very nice to meet you. You look very handsome for the occasion."

Billy grins back.

Touching my arm to get my attention, Aaron nods at the man beside Billy. "This is my best friend,

have our own hockey team that came to town last year. Not that I've ever watched a game, but I know they are an incredible source of pride to our city.

"He is," Aaron replies, watching me carefully.

Then it starts to dawn on me. "And the other guys you introduced me to?"

"All players on the team," he replies.

And then I have an *aha* moment. "And you?"

"First-line defenseman, at your service."

I don't know what that means, but my heart immediately sinks. In the few moments since we arrived, I had been moderately charmed by Aaron and had thought this wouldn't be such a bad date.

But he's a professional athlete, not a part-time jock as I'd thought.

Famous.

And with that comes a whole slew of complications I have absolutely no desire to be embroiled within.

Whatever expression has just come unbidden to my face, Aaron sees it and immediately frowns. "You have something against hockey players?"

"Not per se," I reply truthfully. "I mean… I had a vibe you were a jock. I just didn't realize you were a…"

I struggle to find the right words. Aaron waits patiently.

Shrugging, I say, "A jocky jock."

"That's not even a thing," he scoffs, his eyes twinkling with amusement.

"It's a thing," I say assuredly.

"But it's a problem?" he presses, his hand reaching out to take mine again. "Because I can assure you that you're safe with me."

I shake my head, plastering on a confident smile to put him at ease because I most certainly don't want to talk about my anxieties. Internally, I'm incredibly uncomfortable right now, but I'm not about to let him know it. All I have to do is suffer through this evening and one more wedding next weekend, then I can safely put Aaron Wylde and his fame behind me.

"No, it's fine," I assure him, but I'm not sure how truthful it sounds. "Just caught me by surprise."

◆

IT'S TURNED INTO quite the party—this wedding reception—and while I don't know much about professional sports teams, I can tell it goes far beyond just being a job for these people.

They're all legitimately close to each other, which is saying something given there's twenty-three men on the active roster. Aaron shared that little tidbit with me when I kept meeting player after player and finally asked him how many there were.

He'd laughed—telling me it was adorable how little I knew about the sport. He wasn't surprised, though, telling me that I was not alone. There were lots of people who didn't know a damn thing about hockey, but he was more than happy to teach me whatever I wanted to know.

There was enough double-entendre in that statement I knew he was alluding to other things, and, admittedly, I had a brief moment of regret this was going nowhere because—outside of being famous, rich, and most likely egotistical to the core when drilled deep—he was singularly the most attractive man I'd ever been on a date with.

Not just in the looks department, although his are unparalleled, but he's clearly well-read as we actually spent some of the evening talking books. He's funny as well, which is something I appreciate—no, require—in the opposite sex. I've learned through all kinds of pain and heartbreak that laughter is the key to leading a happy life when all else fails.

So yeah, he's hot, and interesting, and smart, but I just don't think I'd ever be able to get past the fame issue. It's definitely a deal-breaker for me, and I can't believe my luck. I'm just a small-city girl, who spends her days with her nose stuffed in a book. When I had my one awful, horrendous, humiliating brush with fame—at one point believing it to have fully destroyed me—I never thought it would cross my doorstep again.

What are the chances?

Throughout the evening, I'm also introduced to Aaron's teammates' significant others. They're all sweet and incredibly accepting of me. All are surprised to see Aaron with a date and seem incredibly pleased he brought one. Soon enough, I'd figured out Aaron must be the devoutly single dude everyone wants to find true love, but who is resistant to it. This became patently obvious when Tacker's girlfriend, Nora, leaned into him as we were all standing around talking and whispered, "I really like her. Good for you."

I don't think she meant for me to hear it, or maybe she did, but it was definitely clear I'm an anomaly in Aaron's life.

Which actually makes me feel a bit better over the fact I'm going to leave him in the dust after next weekend's wedding.

I do believe the reception would have gone on all night if it weren't for the fact Erik and Blue are catching a late-night flight out for their honeymoon in Australia. Attendants started clearing off the tables and caterers packed away the food, offering little to-go boxes to guests who wanted them.

It takes a while to say our goodbyes. As I'm receiving hugs from the women I'd met and whose names I will never remember for the long run but remember right now—Blue, Brooke, Pepper, Regan, and Nora—I have a moment's regret I'll never be friends with them. I can say they are all genuinely nice and welcoming. As Aaron promised, everyone seems down to earth and humble.

I figure it's an act, or maybe it isn't. Not up to me to figure these people out. It's enough to know they are in a certain class and I'm in a different one, meaning I don't belong.

Aaron leads me out of the house into the warm, dry evening, and we meander over to the valet stand. He walks casually beside me, hands tucked into his pockets. "I assume you wouldn't have any interest in going out for a drink somewhere?"

I give him a small smile. Handing my ticket to the valet, I watch as he rushes off to get my car. "I'm tired. I think I'll call it an evening."

"Going to tell me why you don't like me being a professional athlete?" he asks, still correctly guessing about my discomfort, but not exactly the reasoning behind it.

"Nope," I reply, then try to sugarcoat it a bit so he leaves it alone. "I promise… it's not a big deal."

"Still intend to honor our date next weekend?" he asks.

"Of course," I reply, but there's enough aloofness in my tone he knows it will be our last date.

"Hmmm," he muses and before I know it, he's leaning into me. "Then I'm not going to regret doing this at all."

It's completely unexpected and given my reticence about Aaron and all he represents, it's shocking how quickly I respond to his warm mouth on mine. It's not a goodbye peck thanking me for a wonderful evening.

It's a penetrating kiss that tells me he could show me oh so much more if I'd give him a chance past next weekend.

It's over as soon as it starts, but the tingling of my lips leaves me a pointed reminder left by a sinful man I want to despise, but I really just can't.

As Aaron turns to walk back toward the house, I watch his retreating back, knowing he's going to be on my mind for quite some time.

CHAPTER 5

Wylde

"D UDE... I DON'T understand what you had in all these boxes," I say as I break another one down, pulling the flaps out and flattening it.

I've spent the morning at Kane's condo, helping him clear out the mounds of cardboard he has left from his move. There have to be fifty empty boxes, yet I don't see what he had in them as everything is neatly put away. Nothing out of place.

Kane snickers as he flattens a box out, adding to the pile we'll carry down to my truck and then haul to the dump. "Word of advice... don't open any of the closets in this place."

Now that makes more sense.

"Duly noted." Laughing, I grab another box. "But you got a great place here."

"Thanks, man. Lucked out really."

I'll say. His condo is about the same size as mine in

square feet, but his comes with an amazing outdoor balcony that overlooks downtown with a stunning view of the arena the Vengeance plays in, which is all glass and steel, sparkling in the late afternoon sunset.

"So how did it go with the hot redhead after Erik and Blue's wedding?" Kane asks, giving me a lecherous grin. "Did you score one for the team if you know what I mean?"

I shake my head. "Yeah... I know what you mean and no, I didn't score one for the team."

"What?" he exclaims with exaggerated surprise. "You mean the team's playboy... the man himself who goes by nothing but the moniker Wylde... struck out?"

"Can't strike out if you don't attempt to play," I say with a wink. "Let's just say she's not the type of woman you hookup with."

Kane's expression clouds with confusion. "Look, dude... I get we've only known each other for a few months and all, but I had the distinct impression not only from you, but also from pretty much everyone on this team, you don't do anything but hookups. This girl that special?"

I shrug. "I have no clue what she is other than intriguing. Maybe she's just a challenge for all I know. I'm just rolling with it."

Kane regards me before giving me a smirk. "Famous last words."

"Look," I say, holding my arms out. "I'm not looking for anything serious. This might not be a one-night stand, but it's definitely not a relationship or anything. We've only been on one date."

"And you're taking her to Dax and Regan's wedding this weekend?" he prompts.

"Yup," I tell him.

He seems to consider this. "And have you been with anyone else since you met her?"

That question strikes me, sucking the cockiness right out of my expression. "Well... no."

"And why is that?" he drawls, looking superior and as if he has me all figured out.

I roll my eyes, my voice dripping with sarcasm. "It's not like I screw a different woman every night, Kane. In fact, I've been known to go two, sometimes three, whole days without fucking a woman."

"And yet, it's been at least five days since you first met her and three days since the wedding?" he replies, and I wince at the way he's just called me out.

I play it off with a half shrug. "Just because I'm not interested in fucking someone else doesn't mean I want this chick on a permanent basis."

Because I don't.

And yet... even as I just used the word "chick"—a term I've used in conjunction with women for years—I realize how inappropriate it is to think of Clarke in that way.

She's way more than just some "chick," deserving far better than that from me. It's a moment of growth for me, and I immediately feel the pressing need to correct that. "I didn't mean to call her a chick."

Kane cocks an eyebrow.

"What I mean," I drawl, trying to explain this to him in a way even I might understand, "is she's an intriguing woman whom I'm not only attracted to, but also actually interested in getting to know a bit better. That's all."

He opens his mouth and I can tell by the expression on his face it's to say something smart ass, but he's distracted by his phone ringing. When he pulls it from his pocket, a smile lights up on his face.

Ignoring me, he taps the screen to connect the call, but rather than putting it up to his ear, he focuses on the screen.

Must be FaceTime.

Holding the phone out a bit, his smile turns even brighter when the call fully connects and he can see the person calling. "Hey, Noodle," he exclaims, sheer happiness in his tone. "About damn time you called."

Noodle?

"Whatever," a distinctly young and female voice chides back with a laugh. "You could have called me anytime."

Now I'm curious. I walk around the coffee table where we'd been stacking the cardboard boxes to peek shamelessly over Kane's shoulder.

Holy shit.

Noodle is an absolute hottie. Caramel-brown hair that gets lighter as it falls down away from her face, parted down the middle and hanging over both shoulders, suntanned skin, and blue eyes. I can't see much of the background as she's holding her phone close to her face, but what a face it is.

Kane throws his thumb over his shoulder, knowing I'm right behind him. "That's my teammate, Wylde."

Smiling, I wave from over his shoulder. "Hi, Noodle."

She snorts, white teeth flashing. "It's actually Mollie. Nice to meet you."

"Back at you," I say, then add on with a wink, "Noodle."

I move away to give them face-to-face privacy but have no intention of leaving the room. Grabbing another box to deconstruct, I hear Mollie say, "For Christ's sake, Kane... will you stop calling me Noodle? It's the most ridiculous thing ever."

I wonder who this woman is. Kane doesn't have a sister, just two younger brothers back home in California.

He also doesn't have a serious girlfriend, as we've

had those conversations over the last couple months since he joined the team.

Whoever she is, she's important because his reaction to her just couldn't be tamed.

The conversation is short and easy to follow, the extent of which she's going to be traveling through Arizona in October and wants to visit for a few weeks. They make tentative plans, talk about mutual friends, and he warns her to be careful in her travels.

When he hangs up not five minutes after the call started, I look over the current box in my hand. "Noodle?"

There's a sappy smile that comes to his face. "Yeah... nickname she earned in college one night after she got too drunk at a party and passed out. I had to carry her three blocks back to her apartment, and she was limp as a noodle. And so was born her nickname."

"Aaah," I say in understanding. "Old college flame."

"Nope," he replies with a shake of his head. "Best friend from college."

"Your best friend from college is a woman?" I ask in disbelief. Not that men and women can't be friends. Or best friends for that matter. It's just not common, so it's shocking.

"Best friend period," he corrects. "That number-one spot has remained hers."

I stand there, absolutely still, even more jolted by his

proclamation. I try to reconcile that... two extremely attractive people being only friends.

It's just weird.

"And you and she never..." I let the implication hang there.

A slow smile curves his mouth. "Once... in college. There was alcohol and a bad breakup with her boyfriend. It was a bad choice, and we went back to the friend's only category after."

Taking a step backward, I sit on his couch. I can feel the frown heavy on my face. "I don't get it."

He bends over, picking up a box. "What don't you get?"

"Just... she's gorgeous. You're okay looking for a dude, and you're a professional athlete. People like you two belong in a category other than friends."

"Not true," he counters.

Nope. Not buying it. "You mean to tell me that you're not attracted to her in the slightest?"

He shakes his head, but there's enough of a hesitation there that it confirms all I need to know. "Not interested in her like that."

"That's good to know," I drawl, pushing up from the couch again. "Maybe I'll take a crack at her when she comes to visit in October."

Fury blazes in Kane's eyes, and I can see the struggle on his face as he tries to quell it. "Don't make me kick your ass," he warns in a low voice.

"I knew it," I exclaim, pointing an accusing finger. "You've got it bad for her."

"I do not," he snaps back. "She's just a friend."

"Best friend," I say, correcting his attempt to put her in an unimportant category. "Seriously… what's the deal? You two clearly care for each other."

Kane sighs, dropping the box he was holding and raking his fingers through his hair. "Look… it doesn't matter. We were clearly never meant to be anything but friends—the best of—because here we both are, leading separate lives."

"So change it," I suggest.

"That ship has sailed," he replies glumly. "She's a travel blogger… a nomad. She travels around North and South America in a converted, tricked-out van with her dog, Samson. Her home is on wheels, and she goes where her whims take her. She's not the settling-down type, and I'm not into long-distance relationships."

"But—"

Kane holds his hand up. "Best friends work for us, okay?"

It's clear he doesn't want to talk about it, and I feel bad for the dude. He clearly has it bad for his Noodle, but if what he says is true about her and her nomadic lifestyle, then I don't see how they can be together unless Kane wanted to leave hockey and travel with her.

He still has a lot of career left ahead of him, so I don't see that happening.

On top of that, I have no clue if this woman feels anything for him in return. It could be a moot issue.

Which makes me think about Clarke.

And the way Kane has pointed out that since meeting the woman, I've not shown a single bit of interest in tapping a piece of random ass. I can't figure out why not, because I sure as fuck like sex.

Like having it a lot.

And yet, it's only Clarke I'm interested in right now and while I'd give anything to get her into my bed, that's kind of a secondary goal right now.

Why is that?

I know virtually nothing about her other than she makes my blood race when I'm near her, and she's so very different from any woman I've ever been with. More than anything, I think I'm attracted to the way she's not overtly attracted to me. Yes, that makes her a bit of a challenge, but not in a way I need to win this game.

More like I want to make sure we both win, but first I have to figure out exactly how hard I'm willing to play.

CHAPTER 6

Clarke

"I THINK YOU'RE really going to enjoy this one, Mrs. Gerber." I lovingly wrap one of my favorite books of all time, *The Prince of Tides* by Pat Conroy, in lavender-colored tissue paper, sealing the edge with an oval sticker that says, "Clarke's Corner," and place it in a gift bag.

Mrs. Gerber was one of my very first customers when I opened my door for business, and she comes in at least once a week for a new book. Lately, she's given up control to me to introduce her to new genres and today, I'm passing off a literary genius of a book, in my humble opinion. I've probably read it twenty times, my own paperback copy worn and dog-eared.

"I look forward to it, dear," she replies, handing over her credit card.

While I ring up the transaction, I keep an eye on two female teenagers who came in a few moments ago.

They're lurking in the back row and giggling about something, probably reading snippets from a sexy romance novel or something.

"Now, Clarke," Mrs. Gerber says as she leans across the counter a bit, lowering her voice. "My book club was thinking about branching out of our normal brand to try something new."

"Like what?" I ask. Her book club is made up of little old ladies like herself, who, while they enjoy books, love the social aspect of getting together once a month to nibble on sweetcakes and gossip after their book discussions.

"Oh, I don't know," she replies breezily, waving a hand covered in expensive rings and dotted with age spots. "We were thinking of maybe trying *Fifty Shades of Grey*."

I suck in air so fast I actually end up choking. Mrs. Gerber watches me warily while I pound my own chest and try to apologize through my wheezing.

"*Fifty Shades?*" I manage to gasp, and I notice the two teenagers in the back have gone absolutely silent. I imagine their heads are tilted, ears pointed in our direction so as not to miss anything. "Do you know what the book is about?"

Mrs. Gerber's lips flatten, and she gives me a look that causes me to physically shrink back a bit. "I'm old, Clarke, not dead. Of course I know what it is, and why wouldn't a woman my age be interested in something like that?"

I have no good reply because she's absolutely right, and I was just stereotyping her based on her age. "You know what," I drawl as I move out from behind the counter. I move over to the third row of books, where, lo and behold, the two girls are standing and watching me with wide eyes and slide my finger down a row of books. I find what I'm looking for, grab it, and head back to the counter.

Holding it up for Mrs. Gerber to see, I display a hardback edition of *Fifty Shades* and slide it in her bag. "This one's on the house. How about you read it first? Then, if you think your book club would like it, I can put in an order for them."

Mrs. Gerber beams, and I know, without a doubt, *The Prince of Tides* will not see the light of day for a while.

After I complete the transaction, I walk around the store, making sure nothing has been moved out of place by the browsers who have been in and out today. I've got another two hours before I turn the night shift over to my only other employee, Nina, who has been with me from the start. She's a college student paying her own way through school, and she covers the store for a few hours each evening, Tuesday through Saturday, where we'll close at nine.

Sundays and Mondays, I close at five.

Finally, the two young girls emerge from the stacks, one with two bright splotches on her cheeks carrying a paperback book. I recognize the romance novel from afar, and I find it slightly adorable they're embarrassed to be buying it.

I have no clue the true source of the blushes. It could be they're embarrassed in general to be reading romance, which I think is ridiculous. If this is their first, maybe they'll come back tomorrow and buy more. Maybe it's because it has sex scenes and they'll be getting an education, but Lord knows... I read my mom's when I was about their age and it's how I learned about the birds and the bees.

Maybe it's because they just had a back-row seat to watching an elderly woman requesting *Fifty Shades* and being proud about doing it.

Whatever the reason, I chat them up as I ring up their purchase, telling them if they enjoy the book, I have more recommendations. And, as I tell every new customer before they leave, "Thank you for shopping here, and I'd really love to have you back."

I don't make a rich living off this bookstore, and let's be honest, most of the money I make is from the products I sell other than books. People nowadays are reading on tablets and phones or listening to audio versions. There's just not a lot of the same demand for tangible book products as there used to be, but I love having this little independent slice of heaven for those purists who still flip pages as they read.

The bell on the door jingles as they leave, and I move out from behind the counter to once again start tidying things up.

The door opens again, bells merrily chiming, and I turn to welcome my next customer.

It's a physical jolt to my body to see Aaron Wylde there, all casual, confident, and totally hot.

Totally out of my league.

He has on a pair of cargo shorts, a navy t-shirt, and a pair of flip-flops. His wavy blond hair flops boyishly over his forehead, and there's a layer of stubble across his jawline.

I hadn't heard from him after our wedding date on Saturday other than a text from him later that night asking if I'd made it home okay. When I'd replied I had, he'd merely responded with…

Awesome. I'll see you next Saturday. More info to come.

It had rankled me a bit, to be honest, that it was all I got from him. In fairness, I knew I had not given him any indication to believe I was interested in him in any way, and, to be clear, I am not.

But he'd been so insistent on going out with me—to the point of practically entrapping me into a date—that I expected more effort. That got me to thinking that maybe there's just nothing special about me, so he was taking me saying I wasn't interested at face value.

Which I am most certainly not.

Still, it plays with a girl's confidence.

I'm stunned to see him in my store, just out of the blue. Three days after last seeing him without any communication.

Not that I expected any, because no way am I interested.

Sure… I've thought about him some.

A moderate amount, actually.

Playing over and over in my head everything he'd said, every action he took, on the last Saturday we spent together. I searched my memory and overanalyzed the situation, trying to locate the tell-tale signs of what I termed to be Famed Douche Affliction.

That disease or defect by which people suffering from an unmitigated case of being an asshole because they feel entitled to be such, be it by way of fame or wealth.

I couldn't see it within Aaron, but to be fair he would have been on his best behavior.

Maybe I'll see it now.

"What are you doing here?" I ask, but not in a snotty, unwelcoming way. In a truly surprised, slightly awed kind of way, which is how I'm feeling in this moment.

His teeth flash, expression teasing. "I missed you,

too."

"Never said I missed you," I quip.

"Maybe not, but I happen to know I'm incredibly charming and funny. I'm sure you missed me just a bit."

"'Fraid not," I reply, struggling not to let my lips curl in amusement. He is funny and charming... I'll give him that.

"Actually," he says, turning slightly away from me and facing the bookshelves. "I thought I would come in to purchase a book. I really should make more time for reading."

Aaron walks away, disappearing down the first aisle.

I feel compelled to call out to him in warning, "If you're saying that thinking it will help you get in my pants, I'm telling you it won't."

He makes a scoffing sound, but he doesn't say anything else.

"Need any help?" I ask. Taking a few steps his way, I'm completely unsure as to what to do. If he were an ordinary customer, I'd follow him down the aisle and make a resounding offer of help.

He's not ordinary, though, and I don't want him thinking I'm intrigued in any way.

"I'm good," he calls back, firmly letting me know he does not need or want my attention right now.

Totally confusing.

I resolve myself to ignore his presence—yeah,

right—and move to the opposite side of the shop to tinker with shelves laden with picture frames of all shapes and sizes. I move them around, shifting some forward and others back. Totally useless and unneeded work, my ears straining to hear anything from where Aaron is perusing the books.

I finally decide to do something productive, moving back behind the checkout counter to where my laptop is located. After firing it up, I open my inventory report and start making a list of things I need to order.

After about ten minutes, Aaron eventually comes out from the stacks, holding a book. I can't get a good enough look to identify it. He strolls over to the little reading corner I'd set up, settling down into one of the cushiony chairs there.

He opens the book to the first page. He's chosen not a literary classic as I thought he would, but rather a Dean Koontz book.

One of my favorites... *Intensity*.

I just stare as he reads, carefully flipping the pages. After about the fourth page flip, his eyes drift up and over the edge of the book to lock on me.

Blushing deeply, I try to duck my head to focus on my computer screen, but I'm forced to acknowledge him when he asks, "Is it okay if I sit here and read for a bit?"

"Of course," I reply quickly.

"I was just wondering… since you were staring so hard, I thought I might be doing something wrong."

"Nope," I assure him, with a shake of my head so hard, my glasses almost dislodge from my face. "That's the whole point of the little reading corner. Make sure the book is to your liking before you buy it."

Aaron smirks as his eyes drift back down.

God, why does he have to look so hot sitting there, reading Dean Koontz and totally ignoring me? And to top it all off, I know he's behaving this way so he seems cool and mysterious because he thinks it will pique my interest even more.

That may be true, but I refuse to let him know it.

Aaron sits there for almost twenty minutes, slowly reading—probably savoring and hopefully enjoying—the creepiness of Koontz.

Finally, he pushes out of the chair, then saunters over to the checkout counter. I push my laptop aside, letting my gaze settle on the book in his hand. "So what did you think?"

"It's good," he replies, setting it on the counter. "I'll take it."

"Awesome," I reply brightly, happy to make a sale to compensate for the way he's unsettled me since walking in my store. "Is this your first Koontz?"

"Yup," he replies. "Actually, my first book in a long time. Not sure how I fell so far out of the habit, but let's just say it's been years since I've picked a book up."

"I imagine your dad wouldn't approve of this type of literature given he taught the classics," I say.

The minute the words are out, I know they're wrong by the way Aaron's face clouds over with something I might label as bitterness. But it smooths away just as quickly, making me wonder if I really even saw it.

Aaron doesn't respond to my statement about his dad, but rather catches me totally off guard. "Any interest in grabbing dinner with me tonight?"

"Sorry," I reply as I scan the bar code on the back of the book. "I have plans already."

"Date?" he asks.

"Is that really any of your business?" I reply, feeling my smug expression. Just a bit of payback for him making me feel all out of sorts this afternoon.

Aaron shrugs. "Not really, but I'd just be curious as to my competition."

"I'm not a prize," I retort primly, mainly to hide the fact he is totally charming me with the passive flattery.

Bending slightly, Aaron puts a forearm on the counter and leans in toward me. "You know, given the brush-offs you keep giving me, I'm going to agree... you're no prize."

I blink like an owl, trying to figure out if he's teasing or lobbing a well-designed insult my way. His tone is light, his eyes sparkling with challenge. He doesn't seem mean-spirited, but I know better than anyone that people never show their true faces up front. That usually comes later, after some level of trust is built.

"I must be a glutton for punishment," he intones, straightening his body. "Because I'm bound and determined to get you to like me, Clarke Webber."

Snorting, I place the book in a bag, then nab the credit card he holds out. I decide to throw him a bone. "Well, if it's any consolation, I don't actually dislike you."

"No, you just don't trust me," he replies firmly and now I know he's more than just taking some haphazard stabs at flirting with me. He's incredibly observant and intuitive.

"Sorry," I reply in a tone that doesn't sound at all apologetic. I give a careless shrug as I hand him back the credit card, pushing the receipt he needs to sign across the counter with a pen. "Guess that's a flaw of mine."

Aaron completes the transaction, takes the bag containing his book, and steps back from the counter. "Nothing wrong with being cautious, Clarke. Maybe one day you'll tell me why you take it to the extreme."

"Maybe," I murmur thoughtfully.

He holds up his hand in farewell, turning for the door. "See you tomorrow?"

A lazy smile starts to tug at my lips, then I jerk at the realization of what he just said. "Tomorrow?" I call after him.

He glances over his shoulder, giving me a megawatt smile that causes my stomach to flutter. "I'll be back for another book."

And with that, he disappears out the door.

CHAPTER 7

Wylde

I PULL UP in front of Clarke's small house in the Coronado neighborhood of Phoenix. I consider it a victory I got the address from her, and she allowed me to pick her up for Dax and Regan's wedding.

It took substantial effort on my part. Four straight days of visits to her bookstore, conversations about the books I'd read, and one afternoon where I'd helped her stock books that had been delivered via UPS on the shelves.

But over the course of this week, there was a definite, incremental, warming up on her part. It's not like I put on an act while in her store. It was no hardship to browse through books for an interesting read, then immerse myself in it.

Granted... I wasn't pretending to be something I wasn't. I shamelessly flirted while getting to know her, taking the time in between her waiting on customers to talk about what I'd read the prior night or fish for information about her.

In return, she wasn't playing hard to get, but she still tried to maintain her distance. I figured out soon enough that something happened to her in the past that made her genuinely mistrustful of men. Still, she was like a flower blossoming under my continual attention, opening up petal by petal.

I was able to learn some things about her.

Like she's super smart... double major in English and Communications.

Her favorite classic book is *To Kill A Mockingbird*.

She's originally from San Diego, but her parents moved to Phoenix when she was three. They still live in the area, and she's close to them.

Her best friend is a divorcee who apparently did so well in her divorce settlement she'll never have to work another day in her life. Ironically, she really wants to work, but she can't figure out where her passion lies. I met her one day when she breezed in, wearing couture workout clothes that showed off every curve, with expertly applied makeup and looking like a million bucks.

Still, I preferred Clarke's natural beauty any day of the week.

Best of all, while she was mildly skittish and held herself in reserve at times, Clarke actually gave me the benefit of the doubt in incremental doses as each day wore on, and this was evidenced by her trusting me enough to give me her address so I could pick her up.

Clarke lives in the historic neighborhood of Coronado in a small brick bungalow off 8th Street. I pull to the front of the curb and shut my truck off, enjoying the last moment of air conditioning before I step out in the dry summer heat that usually takes my breath away each time it slaps me in the face.

I exit my truck, round the front, and barely step onto the sidewalk when I see Clarke coming out her front door. She pulls it closed behind her, then locks it.

Waiting at the end of the pathway, I take a moment to check her out. It's another summer wedding so she's in pastel colors. This time, she's in a white dress with large yellow and pink flowers that swishes around mid-calf. She has on a pair of gold sandals with a spiky heel that are actually really sexy.

But true to Clarke's nature to sort of hide herself, she's wearing little makeup, has her hair pulled up on top of her head, and has her glasses lodged on her nose like battle armor. When she turns to face me, she actually pushes them up with her index finger. I want to memorialize that moment forever because it's when I realize Clarke will never be able to hide how gorgeous and sexy she is no matter how hard she tries.

I can't help but tease her as she starts down the

porch steps. "Not going to invite me in?"

My request startles her, and she stumbles a bit on the last step. I'm too far away to make a grab to steady her, but, luckily, she rights herself, once again pushing her glasses up her nose in a move I think is more from habit than anything else.

"What for?" she asks suspiciously.

"Um… because that's sort of polite manners," I say with a laugh. "At the very least, most women wait inside for their date to come up and escort them out."

"I'm not most women," she replies tartly.

"No, ma'am, you are not," I agree wholeheartedly as she reaches me. I take her hand, tuck it into the crook of my elbow, and lead her back to my truck. "May I say you look incredibly lovely this fine evening?"

The sun hangs low in the sky, casting a warm glow all around us and making the bare skin on Clarke's arms shimmer. I feel like instead of a wedding, we should be having a moonlit picnic by a lily-strewn pond while crickets chirp in the background.

Or some romantic shit like that, which is odd, as I'm the least romantic dude in the world. But, for whatever reason, Clarke sort of inspires those thoughts, which is something that freaks me out a bit. I'm way out of my comfort zone here, yet… I'm looking forward to the evening ahead.

When we reach my truck, Clarke looks at it with

apprehension, as even with the running board, it's quite the hike up.

"Your chariot awaits," I advise with a sweep of my arm. Clarke snorts in return.

I open the door, then hold her hand as she delicately puts one sandaled foot on the running board and her other hand on the door. With one tiny bounce, she hoists herself into the seat, primly tucking her dress around her legs as I shut the door.

♦

THE EVENING IS turning out to be a lot of fun, and Clarke's actually letting her hair down a bit, but only in the metaphorical sense. I would kill to actually see it down in its full glory, and I wonder how far it'll hang down her back.

Most of the team also made this wedding as they did last week with Erik and Blue's. In contrast to that one, Dax and Regan decided to have theirs in a small non-denominational church they attend sometimes.

They went traditional on everything, sparing no expense or detail. Some would think it strange, given they'd already been married for several months, but their marriage came about in the most unconventional of manners. Dax married Regan to provide her health insurance as she battles an extremely rare blood disorder. They fell in love after that and now, Dax is giving her the wedding she'd always dreamed about.

At least that's what my best friend Tacker told me, who got it straight from his woman, Nora, who got it from Regan.

Regardless, she has the classic white wedding dress that makes her look like a fairy-tale princess. Dax is dapper in a tuxedo. They don't have a huge contingent of people at their sides. Regan chose Dax's sister, Willow, to be her maid of honor.

Or, rather, I guess it's matron of honor as Willow eloped to Vegas with the team's owner, Dominik Carlson, the day after the Vengeance won the Cup. They've since been on an extended honeymoon in the Maldives, having just made it back yesterday to attend this wedding.

Dax chose Legend Bay, our team's goalie, to be his best man, which caused a good-natured argument among Bishop and Erik, who both felt they were equal candidates. They were still grumbling about it ten minutes ago when I went to get refills on drinks for Clarke and me.

The reception is at some ritzy country club Dax and Regan don't belong to, but who will rent out their facilities to a Vengeance superstar with no qualms. They went over the top with a surf-and-turf dinner, open bar, and live band for us to dance away to all evening long.

The one similarity to Erik and Blue's wedding is

Dax and Regan also have the Cup at their wedding reception, which they filled with champagne and dipped glasses in for their first toast.

Clarke and I are seated at a table with Tacker, Nora, Bishop, and Brooke for the meal. Erik and Blue are not here as they're still away on their honeymoon. Legend and Willow, along with their partners, sat at the bride and groom's table.

Since the meal has concluded, most people mingle around in between band sets of the finest cover songs, switching up tables to sit and chat. The traditional bride-and-groom dance has been completed with Peter Frampton singing *Baby, I Love Your Way*.

Clarke is currently at our table beside Pepper and Willow, and she's engaged in an animated discussion. Pepper is an author and writes children's stories. Willow is a photojournalist. I figured they'd both get along with Clarke, and I see I'm correct.

It was cool this past week when I'd found one of Pepper's books on the shelves in Clarke's store while I was browsing, and she'd freaked out I knew the author. On the way to the wedding, Clarke asked me if she thought it would be tacky if she asked Pepper to do a signing at the store. I assured her it would not. I'm confident Pepper would be glad to do it.

The men have vacated the table, but we're all standing in a cluster right beside it, reliving some of the Cup championship game, because yes... three weeks since the win and we're still riding the high.

A slow song starts playing—one I frankly don't recognize—but Tacker turns his back on me in midsentence, then pulls Nora up from the table, interrupting a conversation she was having with Brooke.

I glance over at Clarke. I haven't had a moment alone with her since we got here. This reception proved to be about the worst place to take a date since it's such a social event, and Clarke had met most of the people last weekend. She's a natural extrovert, which I witnessed all week at her store as she greeted customers and carried on interesting conversations with them. She's spent most of the evening talking with the women—Willow being the only one Clarke hadn't met last weekend.

But watching Tacker pull Nora in close to him for a dance, I realize I have the perfect opportunity for some alone time with Clarke. I haven't forgotten she made it clear she's only in this for the two dates I won from her.

I move around the table, come up behind Pepper so Clarke sees me, and gift her with a charming smile. Her eyes rise to meet mine, causing Pepper and Willow to shift to see what has her attention.

I hold my hand out. "Would you like to dance?"

I half expect her to say, "not really," which could very well be a joke, or, equally as plausible, could be the truth. To my pleasant surprise, she places her hand in mine and gracefully pushes out of her chair.

The weight of stares as I lead her to the dance floor is palpable. Tonight, almost every one of my teammates has managed to pull me aside or catch me away from Clarke to inquire about being seen with the same woman more than once. I took a ton of ribbing from the guys, and I got a lot of sappy, romantic looks from their women. Brooke even managed to corner me to tell me how much she likes Clarke, and how she hopes we'll be happy together.

I didn't have the heart or the guts to tell them Clarke doesn't really want to be here, has some sort of grudge against men, and I'll most likely never see her again.

But at least I have this dance right now.

The floor fills up with other couples, and I lead Clarke right to the middle. As a defenseman, I can be rough and tumble on the ice, but I've always been a smooth dancer. While I love clubbing and dancing to a much faster beat, there's nothing wrong with a slow dance and a beautiful woman held captive in my arms.

It's the closest Clarke and I have been physically since we've met. I take advantage of the situation to wrap my arm completely around her, pulling her in close. When I take her hand in mine, she rests hers on my shoulder.

At first, as we're swaying, she doesn't look at me. Pretending to be interested in her surroundings, she averts her eyes to the side, smiling at those who dance around us. That's fine by me—at least for a bit. I don't mind looking at her. Even with her glasses covering a good chunk of her face, there's still plenty to stare at that's awfully pretty.

"So…" I finally drawl, trying to get her attention. She swings her gaze up. "Are you really going to stick to your guns and refuse to go out with me past this date?"

She blinks in surprise. "You mean you want to go out with me again?"

She sounds so stunned I take a quiet, reflective moment to ascertain if I truly do. The question was sort of spontaneous and now that I think about it, I have to wonder why I would want to.

Clarke has kept me at arm's length, only opening up in bits and pieces. I had to essentially force her to go out with me, and at this moment, I don't even see sex as an option any time soon. Which, let's face it, is my primary motivator in taking a woman out.

And yet, I find myself admitting, "I'd very much like to take you out again. Without having to win it from you on a dare or a bet."

Her gaze slides away from mine, and she looks around the room. Chewing on her lower lip, she thinks about my offer. I can tell it's this environment that has her doubting if she should.

"Hey," I say, putting my fingertips to her chin and forcing her eyes to mine. "Why don't you tell me about whatever it is that's holding you back? I know there's something in particular."

Her eyes move to mine, and in a moment of brutal honesty I wasn't expecting, she says, "Something happened to me in the national limelight by someone famous. It was incredibly hurtful and completely humiliating. Unfortunately, because of that experience, I tend to lump all famous people—celebrities, sports stars, what have you—into the same deceitful category. I know it's not right. It's not fair. But I just have incredible reservations about getting involved with someone who has the power to hurt me like that again."

I am so stunned I actually stop moving. My feet plant solidly on the dance floor, my hands finding my way to Clarke's waist to hold her still. "What happened?" I ask, the concern in my tone evident.

She lets out a deep sigh, shaking her head. "I really don't want to get into it here—"

Enough said. Taking her hand, I lead her from the dance floor.

"Where are we going?" she asks, almost needing to jog to keep up with my long strides.

"Somewhere private where we can talk," I say, moving right to our table so we can grab her purse.

Brooke, Pepper, and Willow are still sitting there, and they smile when we approach. I'm not sure what they see in my expression, but Pepper asks, "Is everything okay?"

I offer a confident smile, but I'm on edge over Clarke's ominous words. Even though I barely know her and have no clue what happened to her, I'm already planning the death of the man who hurt her.

Strange.

"Everything's fine," I assure Pepper, pulling Clarke into my side. "We're just going to head out. Go somewhere for a cup of coffee."

All three women regard us with blank expressions, probably wondering if I've gone off the deep end since it's unlikely Aaron Wylde ever had a cup of coffee with a woman unless it was before kicking her out of his bed in the morning.

"See you around," Clarke says to the women.

"I'll come by your store next week," Pepper promises. "We'll talk about setting up a signing."

"I'd love that," Clarke replies with gratitude.

"Give Dax and Regan our regards, regrets, whatever you call it," I mutter, grabbing Clarke's tiny purse and handing it to her. Then her hand is in mine, and we're making our way out of the country club to find a private place to talk.

CHAPTER 8

Clarke

THE GREATER PART of me doesn't want to tell Aaron about what happened. It's so humiliating and painful I'm sick to my stomach right now even thinking about it.

But something happened this week with Aaron's repeated visits to my store, sometimes to just quietly sit in my presence, that changed something in me. It made me realize Aaron's not just out to score. I mean... look at the man. He could crook his finger... and a hundred gorgeous women would come running. I made the mistake of googling him one night, hoping to learn a bit about the sport he played, and I ended up learning stuff about him that I wish I hadn't.

He's what would be considered the team's player. While many of the Vengeance players are in committed relationships, Aaron's the leader of the single guys. I don't know how many photos I found of him online, all with different women.

What I took from it, though, is I do believe he's genuinely interested in me. And because of that, I feel I owe him the truth of why nothing will probably ever come of this, because I'm not sure I can ever trust him. I want him to know it's not him... it's me.

So I'm going to swallow my pride, dredge up the horrific memories, and lay it out straight.

Wylde keeps a hold of my hand as we leave the country club. He helps me into his massive truck and when he settles into the driver's seat, he starts the engine and asks, "Where do you want to go so we can talk?"

Smiling, I nod at his dashboard. "Crank that A/C. We can just sit here and talk."

"Don't mind finding a bar for a drink or a coffee shop for some java if you want," he suggests.

"Actually... I don't want to be in public when we talk about this because it's not pleasant for me," I explain.

"And you don't want to be a snotty mess around other people?" he guesses.

I give him a sharp look. "I don't cry over this. Not anymore. That still doesn't make it pleasant, and it's definitely not a conversation I'd have while sipping coffee or wine."

Duly chastised, Aaron's expression turns somber. "I'm sorry. I didn't mean to make light—"

"No," I blurt out, reaching out to touch his arm. "I'm sorry. I shouldn't have snapped at you. But, as you can see, this entire thing sort of gets me riled up."

Aaron studies me before settling back against the driver's door so he can more fully face me. With a sweep of his hand, he says, "Then just go ahead and get it out. Let's talk right here in the privacy of my truck, and you can have whatever emotions you want knowing only I will see them and take them to my grave."

My lips press into a grim smile. "I wish you hadn't turned out to be so nice," I mutter. "You make this even more difficult."

He just smiles, indicating his patience to hear my entire story. I take a deep breath, then dive into my pain.

"You know the show *Celebrity Proposal*?" I ask. The blankness on his face gives me the answer, so I take a moment to explain it. "It's a popular network show where a famous single celebrity dates several common women with the goal being to fall in love and hopefully end up proposing to one."

Aaron's brow furrows deeply. "Are you serious?"

"Unfortunately, I am serious," I reply dryly. "It's like one of the top-watched shows in TV history. It's sort of this whole pauper-to-princess type of mentality. That an average woman can hook a prince—or, in modern-day America, a celebrity."

Didn't think it was possible, but Aaron's eyebrows draw even closer together. "You know, it's not lost on me that exactly describes you and me... not that I would consider you 'common' in any way, but I get what you're saying about what this show tries to do."

I nod, twisting my fingers around one another. "Exactly. At any rate, I was invited to be on the show. My friend Veronica and I auditioned on a lark, and I really thought she'd get picked because even though I said these women are common and average, they really aren't. They're the most beautiful and gorgeous regular American women they can find."

"You're beautiful and gorgeous," he points out. "Granted... in a nonconventional, stand-out-in-a-crowd kind of way."

Aaron doesn't realize he's pretty much hitting the nail on the head on why I was chosen, and subsequently humiliated, but I'm too flattered by the fact he finds me beautiful to call him on it.

"At any rate, I was young, stupid, and totally taken in by the producers when they invited me to be on the show. I was hesitant at first, but then easily seduced by their promises it would be the experience of a lifetime and true love always wins, etc. I was quite the romantic then."

If Aaron can't tell by the bitterness in my voice, I'm not that romantic woman anymore.

"So you went on the show?" he guesses.

"Yeah," I mutter, looking at my hands. "It was basically ten women, and we all lived in a house together. The celebrity single took us out on group dates, then single dates, and each week, he cut one woman from the show."

Aaron winces. "Ouch."

A laugh bubbles out. "Yeah... I thought I'd be one of the first to go. I didn't look like the other women. Didn't act like them. Was quiet. Didn't demand attention. Wanted to discuss politics, not fashion. I didn't fit in at all."

"I'm going to guess you didn't get cut right away." I can hear the slight bit of dread in his voice. He knows something bad happened, just not how bad.

"I made it down to the final four," I murmur, once again not able to hold his gaze. "And when you make it to that point, you go on an 'overnight' date where, as the producers told us, things might get... um... intimate... which was good for ratings, so we shouldn't hold back."

Aaron shifts uncomfortably in his seat, but there's no turning back for me. I have to tell him the rest of the ugly.

I lift my head, locking eyes with him. "Just so you know, it wasn't a game. I had real feelings for this guy, and I thought he returned them. It truly felt that way."

"Let me save you some pain in retelling this," Aaron offers. "I'm going to guess you two got intimate, then it didn't work out."

Oh, if only it were that simple. "I gave him my virginity."

Aaron stiffens, his frown turning downright scary.

"And, as you might guess, he cut me from the show. But that's not even the humiliating part."

"Not sure I want to know anymore," Aaron growls.

Too bad. He needs to understand. "The very night I was cut from the show, he went out with friends. Got drunk and told them all about our evening together. That I was a virgin, didn't know what I was doing, and was so awful there was no way he could keep me around. He even told them he never wanted to keep me past the first round... that I would have been the first cut, but the producers pressured him to keep me so the below-average women would stay involved with the show. That I was good for ratings."

"Son of a fucking bitch," Aaron snarls. "But how do you know he did all that?"

"Because one of his friends recorded him. After the show concluded, it hit all the celebrity news gossip rags. And even though he chose another one of the women— actually proposed and married her later—I became the big news story from that season of *Celebrity Proposal*. There's even an awful meme someone made using my picture floating around. It's a still shot of when he announced he was cutting me. I'd made this terrible face… and they captioned it: *It could be worse. You could have had an overnight with Clarke.*"

"That is the sickest shit I've ever heard," Aaron exclaims hotly. "Who is this fucking douche we're talking about?"

"Tripp Horschen," I mutter.

"Who?" he demands.

I shake my head. "He was a soap-opera actor. Did a few movies."

"Can't be all that famous," Aaron mutters.

"I'd never heard of you," I point out, and he snorts. "The fact is, he became far more famous after that. For being the guy who bagged the awful virgin. I became a cautionary tale to men all over the world, warning them virgins were totally overrated and lousy lays. I became a freaking meme."

"I wouldn't know," Aaron says in a low voice, his gaze moving out the window before coming back. "How long ago was this?"

"Almost three years ago."

"Bet it feels like yesterday, huh?" he sympathizes, and his words endear Aaron to me more than anything else could. That he probably understands how traumatizing it was for me.

I don't bother affirming that, as I'm sure he knows

how much it still affects me based on how squirrely I've been with him. "I'm really sorry, but I just have this horrible, deep-seated distrust of men now. Add to the fact you're a celebrity—I blame part of his behavior on his entitled actor attitude—and well, this was just never going to go anywhere and I wanted you to know the truth about why."

"I understand," Aaron murmurs, reaching over to take my hand. "I'm really sorry that happened to you, and while I should be mad you would lump me into a category with that guy, I understand where you're coming from."

I let out a sigh of relief, and at the same time, I feel strangely let down. I fully expected this tale to send Aaron running for the hills, which is why I let him see my pain. I wanted to let him down easy, so I could go on my way.

But hearing his acceptance of my reasoning, without a proclamation he'd like to keep trying with me, makes me a bit sad at the same time. It's almost like I want my cake and to eat it, too, which is so not cool.

Once more, Aaron squeezes my hand and lets it go. Straightening in his seat, he puts his seat belt on. "Well… it's been a long night. Let me get you home."

"That sounds good," I murmur, reaching for my own seat belt.

We ride in absolute silence to my home, and it gets

more awkward as each mile ticks away.

Aaron pulls up to the curb in front of my house, putting the truck in park but leaving it running. "Let me help you out," he says before jumping out of his side.

I wait for him to come around, then he offers me a gallant hand as I climb down as gracefully as I can in sandaled heels. He even escorts me up the sidewalk to my porch. Pulling the keys out of my clutch, I turn to face him.

"Thanks for understanding."

"Thanks for telling me the story," he replies before bending and placing a quick kiss on my cheek. "I'm sorry that happened to you."

I can do nothing but nod, a strange lump in my throat.

Tears prick at my eyes when he gives me one last smile as he heads to his truck.

And just like that, Aaron Wylde is no more.

CHAPTER 9

Wylde

WHISTLING AS I saunter down the sidewalk, I feel the joy in my day. I'd gotten up and hit the gym for leg day, then pushed myself with a five-mile run. Took a long hot shower, then made a breakfast of eggs, broccoli, and cheddar cheese. Ate an apple for the hell of it.

It was midmorning and hot as hell when I decided to take a stroll around the downtown area. Hit up a coffee shop I'd noticed before and I'm not disappointed with my order. The iced brew hits the spot, and I can feel the caffeine magically percolating in my veins.

I browse in windows as I walk the streets, taking my time to see what this area has to offer. Then I casually cut left, pushing open the door of *Clarke's Corner*. The bells toll sweetly, as if they knew I'd be coming in.

My eyes immediately lock on Clarke, standing be-hind the register as she checks out a customer. Offering her a smile, I move into the stacks, eager to pick out my next read. I take a bit of joy, even, in that shocked, disbelieving look she just shot me.

As if she'd seen a ghost.

Since I started visiting Clarke's store regularly, I've fallen back into a love of reading. Given I'm on vacation with no real obligations other than getting back into a good fitness routine, I've been reading every book I've bought from her cover to cover. I'm ready for a new read today, and I'm considering giving *Harry Potter* a try. I'll make a note to ask Clarke her thoughts on it before I actually make the purchase.

I get lost in scanning the books while sipping at my iced coffee. A few minutes later, I hear the bells go off. I assume the customer she was waiting on had left, and I don't see anyone else in the store.

True enough, her head soon pops around the end of a bookcase, then the rest of her body follows. "What are you doing here?" she asks tentatively.

"Need a new book," I reply, my focus on an interesting-looking book. I pull it out, then hold it up. "John Grisham. Is he any good?"

"I like some of his stuff," she replies stiffly.

I turn to her. "I was thinking about *Harry Potter*. What's your take on that series? Worth my time to get invested in?"

She blows out a frustrated breath, auburn bangs

flying upward briefly before settling back down around her lovely eyes enshrined behind her glasses. "Seriously, Aaron... what are you doing here?"

I put the Grisham book back, then turn to walk two paces so I'm toe to toe with her. "Why wouldn't I be here? Did you think that little confession last night was going to scare me off?"

Instead of being cowed, she lifts her chin in defiance. "Actually, I did."

"You were wrong then," I reply with a grin, teasingly tapping the end of her nose with my finger. "But I am seriously considering *Harry Potter* as my next read and, well, it so happens the girl I'm dating owns a bookstore."

"We are not dating," she replies huffily, trying to push past me.

Her shoulder brushes against mine, the feeling electric and pulsating. I wonder if she feels it, too, but regardless... she's not walking away from me. I grab her arm, stop her trajectory, and spin her back.

Clarke gasps, her cheeks flushed, and fuck... now I want to kiss the hell out of her. Instead, I ask, "Dinner tonight? Pick you up at seven?"

Her confidence ebbs, and her gaze cuts away. "Aaron... I told you, I can't—"

"You can," I interject. "You can try. You can give me a try... a chance. I know what you've been through, so I know the perils. I may be a celebrity, but I hope you know I'm not a douche like that Tripp asshole."

"Aaron," she murmurs, her eyes finally lifting to meet mine. They are filled with fear.

I dip my face closer to hers. "I'm going to let you in on a little secret, okay?"

Clarke nods mutely.

"I'm usually not a prince," I admit bluntly. "I've never dated the same woman more than once or twice. You ask any member on my team, and they'll say I'm a player."

Clarke narrows her eyes. "Why would you even admit that?"

"Because I want you to know I'm being as honest with you as I can," I say. "You have baggage, and I don't know what the fuck I'm doing. This is probably fated for disaster. But I like you, Clarke. I want to get to know you better. It's a first for me, and well… if you give me a chance, it will be like a first for you, too. At least the first in a few years. We can stumble through this together. A joint effort. What do you say?"

She stares, her entire body almost vibrating with skepticism. I can actually feel the tension within her, like a rabbit ready to bolt.

But I've said my part. If she doesn't have it in her to take the chance, I can't hold it against her. The woman was traumatized, and she has every right to go running and screaming away from me.

Then something changes. I can feel her body relax, her brow smooths, and she gives me a tentative smile. "You plead a good case. You can pick me up at seven."

Oh, how I want to kiss her now, but it's not the right time. I mean, it *would* be the right time in a spontaneous way, but I'm not sure if she's ready for that side of Aaron Wylde yet.

"Here or at your house?" I ask to confirm.

"My house," she replies.

"Perfect. Now, how about you help me pick out a book. *Harry Potter*... yes or no?"

"Yes," she concludes, turning her back on me. I follow her into another stack to find her holding up a paperback of *Harry Potter and the Sorcerer's Stone*. Her gaze drops to my iced coffee. "And I'll take a latte next time."

"Noted," I reply with a grin. I tuck that information away, along with all the other things I'm starting to learn about Clarke.

◆

I DON'T STICK around at Clarke's store for too long. She's all business when I'm there. While the first two chapters of *Harry Potter and the Sorcerer's Stone* was interesting, I actually had some other things to do before our date tonight.

Errands included stopping at the dry cleaners to pick up some clothes, grocery shopping, and a quick detour to GNC to stock up on some protein powder Kane had recommended I try.

With a few hours before I need to hop in the shower to get ready for what I'm considering my first real date with Clarke, I putter around my condo. Clearly, I could relax with my new book, but something has been knocking around in my head since I first met Clarke a little over a week and a half ago.

While meeting her was quite the reward for stumbling into her little store, renewing my love of reading brings about some uneasy feelings.

It's true my father was an English professor who inspired my love of reading, particularly the classics. But he also created an ultimate hate of books, one that caused me to abandon them for years.

Without much thought for what I'm about to do, I head into one of the guest bedrooms where I have some boxes packed up in the closet. I'm not one for sentimentality, so I don't keep a lot of stuff. I'm the opposite of a packrat, so when I moved to Phoenix from Dallas this year, I used the opportunity to de-clutter even more.

But there's one box I've been carrying around my entire adult life, and it has remained sealed the entire time. It seems weird now to keep it closeted away since Clarke has reinvigorated my desire to read.

I pull the box off the top shelf, then carry it over to the bed. There are no markings on it, just brown packing tape that's peeling at the edges. Without hesitation, I pull it off and carefully open the top flaps. I half expect an army of spiders to come crawling out, but, when I peer in, it's nothing but what I had packed away ten years ago.

The last remnants of my relationship with my father.

Reaching in, I pull out a stack of books. The paper is yellowed, not because they aged greatly in ten years, but because they were already old when I packed them.

I sift through them, setting them one by one on the mattress. All are classics that were owned by my dad when he was a young man just in high school himself. His favorites, which he read over and over again.

The Count of Monte Cristo.

The Great Gatsby.

1984.

Of Mice and Men.

Lord of the Flies.

Great Expectations.

I've read them all on more than one occasion, hoping to ferret out some nugget of information that would help me understand my father. I'd memorized the lines he'd underlined with a pencil, hoping it would provide a connection to him.

Reaching back in the box, I pull out another book—*Catcher in the Rye*. I can't help but smile as I remember the look on Clarke's face when I was able to identify a quote from it. My ability to do so made me realize I had pushed away all of this great literature because I was angry at my dad, but all it did was hurt me.

While I've been buying modern works from Clarke's store, I decide my goal for the upcoming hockey season is to read one of these old classics a week.

I reach in again, retrieving another book. *The Canterbury Tales*.

My nose wrinkles as I set this one in a different pile. I didn't enjoy Chaucer the first time I read it, so I know I won't now.

The next book that comes out causes a throbbing in the center of my chest, so much so I rub at it with my knuckles.

I stare down at a weathered copy of *The Picture of Dorian Gray* by Oscar Wilde. Flipping to the first page, I start to read Wilde's preface, in which he defended the merits of his work.

The artist is the creator of beautiful things.

Sometimes true, but other times not. For example, I hate Chaucer while others find his work sublime.

Whatever.

The point being, when I first picked out this book from my father's office, which was a converted second-floor bedroom in our house, I was just ten years old. My father was at his desk, reading through mid-term papers, and I'd held it up. "Can I read this one?"

My dad glanced up, reaching for the glass of bourbon he'd been drinking from, and frowned. His words were drunk and slurred. "You'd never be able to really comprehend it at your age. Maybe in a few years."

That was his answer about most of his favorite books I wanted to read, and when I was finally old enough to read and appreciate them, I found he had been correct. Most of this stuff would bore a ten-year-old horribly, so I'd stuck to books such as *The Adventures of Tom Sawyer* to hold my interest.

By the time I finally read *The Picture of Dorian Gray* and was able to understand and have an intelligent discussion about it, my father was no longer around. He'd already abandoned my mother and me, moving on with a new family.

It didn't stop me from trying to have a relationship with him. I used the classic books he'd left behind as a means to bridge the gap. I'd call him, excited to tell him about a passage that captivated me, but he wasn't interested in discussing any of it with me. He'd cleaned his act up. Stopped drinking. Had a pretty new wife and a new daughter he doted on. He had no time for a fourteen-year-old boy who wanted to talk about the social injustices I'd learned about from reading George

Orwell or my fifteen-year-old self who couldn't contain my pride at having finished the gargantuan tome of *Anna Karenina*.

He simply didn't care anymore.

It took years for me to realize that. I valiantly tried to reconnect with the now-sober man, refusing to be bitter I had only ever had the drunk. Refusing to cry over the fact he wouldn't share anything, no matter how small, with his only son whom he'd left behind.

After I graduated high school, but before entering college, I'd packed all these books away and never looked at them again. Once, I'd even considered burning the damn things, but I decided to keep them as a reminder that not all parents are good and loving.

I wonder what Clarke's parents are like. Did they raise her in a way to make her close herself off from men after one bad decision? Not to downplay what that douche did to her, because that was some traumatizing shit. But did her environment make her inherently closed off, thus making my job harder?

And what, exactly, is my job? I mean, what in the hell am I doing with her? Flirting with her, being romantic, flattering her?

Taking her out to dinner? Giving her pecks on the cheek?

That's not me.

Or, at least, it didn't use to be.

The one thing I'll admit is she has opened something up within me. For the first time, I'm interested in a woman for more than just sex. Don't get me wrong… I very much want to have sex with Clarke. Don't think I won't work hard for it, too, probably starting tonight.

But I'm also cool with sticking to the long game for now because she's just that intriguing.

And while her story about what happened on that reality TV show should probably have any sane guy running in the opposite direction, it makes her even more fascinating.

Just as I wonder about Clarke's family and how much of that experience weighs on who she is today, I have to wonder about my own background. Drunk father who didn't give a damn about his wife or son, so much so he happily started a brand-new life without us. Apathetic mother—also a drunk—who didn't care enough to fight for her husband or console her son when his dad left. It left me to raise myself pretty much on my own.

It meant I had to figure out what love meant, along with the boundaries between right and wrong, on my own.

I know it's definitely had to have some effect on my desire—or, let's be honest, lack thereof—to form attachments.

Mostly, I wonder if any of that's going to come back

to haunt Clarke at some point. Am I destined to end up hurting her because I don't have much inside of me to give a woman like her?

I guess only time will tell.

CHAPTER 10

Clarke

M Y PHONE RINGS, causing me to jerk. My finger touches the edge of the curling wand I'm holding in my hair, and I swear I hear my skin sizzle.

"Shit," I exclaim, pulling the wand from my hair and setting it on my bathroom counter. My middle knuckle on my left hand has a small, red welt.

My phone continues to ring, and I look down to see it's Veronica. I tap the screen to connect the call, then immediately set it to speakerphone. "I really don't have time to talk," I drawl, picking up the wand and wrapping another long lock around it.

"You sound panicked," she replies with a chuckle. "Relax… it's just dinner."

Oh, it's so much more than that. I'm going out with a man who knows the truth about my entire sordid, humiliating past, and he doesn't seem to care about it.

I deflect, though, because I don't feel like getting

into it with my bestie just now. Instead, I ask, "How are things on your end?"

"It's going fine," she replies. "Going to be turning the ship over to Nina any moment now."

Veronica covered the store for me this afternoon, after insisting I should go get a mani and pedi before my date. She'd also said, "And when you shower, make sure you shave. Everywhere."

I blew her off. "I am not having sex with him tonight," I'd said with a staunch lift of my chin.

And just to drive home my resolve, I refused to even shave my legs just a bit ago when I showered. I'm wearing a jumpsuit with flowing pants so I can get away with the stubble. It will ensure my clothes stay on all evening, even if Aaron tries to persuade me otherwise.

I'm sure he will. I mean, while he's been a complete gentleman since I've met him, I know tonight is different. He got me to willingly go on a date with him, which puts us in different territory.

It's not as if I'm opposed to sex. I've had a lot of it over the last few years, and I've enjoyed it. My first experience with Tripp Horschen was a disaster, but contrary to what he told the world in his drunken rant on video, it was mostly due to his own inadequacies. Simply put, he doesn't care if a woman experiences pleasure. He's a fumbling oaf who's only interested in getting himself off. I'm sure anyone can imagine what a horrid experience that would be for a virgin.

But I digress.

Bottom line, I've learned a lot since that first time, and I find sex to be quite enjoyable. Not earth-shattering by any means, but fun.

Still, I don't just fall into bed with men. I have to go out with them a few times, start to feel comfortable with them. I have to actually like and respect them to get naked. It's just an integrity thing with me. So all that being said, sex with Aaron is not happening tonight. It's too soon.

"Did you shave?" Veronica asks.

"Nope," I say with a grin into the mirror. I've already done my makeup, and, I have to say, I look pretty good. I don't wear it a lot… usually only if I go out at night, much preferring not to mess with it at all. But I did a dark gray on my eyes, smoky underneath, and my lashes are so long they'll rub against my glasses.

Hmmm.

I set the wand down, then grab my glasses off the sink. They're only needed for reading—progressive bifocals, actually. I put them on and, sure enough, my lashes with my extra-thick formula mascara rub irritatingly against the lenses.

"Crap," I mutter, taking them off.

"What?" Veronica asks.

"I'm going to have to put my contacts in and I haven't worn them in so long they're probably going to irritate my eyes all night."

"But Aaron will be able to see your lovely eyes up close. They're by far your best feature."

"Gee, thanks," I reply dryly, curling the last lock of hair that needs a spiral. "I thought it was my keen intellect and humor."

"Yeah, maybe if you were sixty years old, widowed, and looking to score a new man at that age."

She has a point.

I remove the wand, turn it off, and set it down, giving myself a comprehensive look in the mirror. "Okay... on a scale of one to ten, I think I'm a solid eight tonight."

"You take off a point for hairy legs?" Veronica asks.

My voice is sullen. "No."

"Then you're a seven," she says confidently, and I can't help but let my laughter fill my small bathroom. "But seriously... here's my pep talk. Have a great time, okay? We both know sex isn't happening with hairy legs and pits, but you better come out of it with at least a hot kiss or two to tell me about, okay?"

"Got it," I reply, snapping off a salute she can't see. "Call you when I get home?"

"I'll be waiting," she says, then blows a kiss into the phone before disconnecting.

I glance at the time, realizing I have less than five

minutes before Aaron is due to arrive. Grabbing some lip gloss, I slather a bit on and pucker my lips.

Then I lunge for my small linen closet beside the toilet, scrounging for a box of contacts. It's been weeks since I wore them, and I hope this doesn't spell disaster. Worst-case scenario, I'll bring my glasses as back up, and I'll deal with the irritation of my lashes smudging up my lenses if need be.

When the doorbell finally rings, I've been so busy with last-minute touches I haven't even had time to get nervous. It hits me now, though, with a massive tilt to my stomach and a moment of nausea.

I swallow it down, remembering how sweet Aaron was when I told him about my great humiliation and how persistent he was in seeking a date with me. While I'm still skittish and wary, he's proven to be nothing more than a nice—albeit famous—guy so far. It still scares me a bit, but it isn't debilitating.

I dash through my small house and open the front door, realizing I forgot to put my shoes on. My first look at Aaron causes my breath to catch, and I wonder if I'll ever get used to his level of hotness. He told me to dress semi-casually. He's wearing navy dress slacks and a golf shirt with the Vengeance logo on it. It fits his large frame well, stretching across his broad expanse of chest and fitting oh so snugly around his thick biceps.

His hair is brushed back from his face, a slight wave

held in place with gel, and he's clean-shaven. I take a small sniff, and damn… whatever cologne he's wearing smells good.

Only after I thoroughly ogle him do I finally look up and notice he's checking me out to the same degree. There's something on his face I've not seen before. He's told me I'm pretty—beautiful, actually—but he's never seen me with my hair down or evening makeup applied. My auburn hair falls in gentle waves around my shoulders, stopping halfway down my back. I disagree with Veronica, considering my hair my best feature.

My jumpsuit is straight out of Veronica's closet, same as the last two outfits I'd worn on my dates with Aaron. It's not like I don't appreciate nice clothes or enjoy buying them, but it's kind of useless to do so when my bestie is a super-rich divorcee fashionista who wears the same size as I do.

"You look amazing," Aaron says in a low, overly appreciative voice that causes the hair on my arms to stand on end.

"You look very handsome yourself," I admit, feeling foolish for saying it. It sounds trite when he looks beyond handsome, but if I don't shut up about it now, I'm likely to start blabbering. So instead, I snag my purse off the table in the foyer and announce brightly, "I'm ready to go if you are."

Aaron cocks an eyebrow, a tiny smirk on his lips.

His eyes travel down my body slowly, landing on my feet. "Pretty sure they won't serve us if you're not wearing shoes."

"Crap," I mutter, slapping my palm to my forehead. "Guess I'm a little nervous."

"Would it help if I tell you I'm nervous, too?" he suggests.

I step back from the threshold, inviting him in with a sweep of my arm. "Are you really?"

"Actually, no," he replies truthfully, stepping inside my small living room. He looks around with interest, remarking, "Your house is great, and I love this neighborhood."

"It actually belongs to my parents," I say, closing the door. "One of their rental properties. And I'm sure quite a humble abode from what you're used to."

The minute the words are out of my mouth, I regret them. My tone was patronizing, and while it's an inherent distrust of all things bright and shiny that has anything to do with fame and fortune, Aaron doesn't deserve to have me judge him like that.

He doesn't respond, which immediately has me apologizing. "I'm sorry. That was a bitchy thing to say."

"It's fine, Clarke," he assures me, then makes a shooing motion. "Go get your shoes or we'll be late for our reservation."

I hide my grimace until my back is turned, bolting

to my bedroom for the sexy sling-back shoes Veronica loaned me.

Shit. We're off to a great start, and it appears I might be unwittingly sabotaging my evening with Aaron. At the rate I'm going, I figure I'll have him run off for good by the main course.

"I'M GLAD TO finally see you relaxing," Aaron observes, his fingers playing at the base of his wineglass. He'd ordered a bottle of red after consulting with me to check my preferences. He even had the sommelier pour me a taste when the bottle was opened and presented to Aaron for approval.

I pick up my own glass, take a small sip, and relish the robust taste of the pinot noir he'd chosen. I'm by no means an expert, but I do love trying new wines.

"The wine has helped as has the excellent meal we just ate," I admit with a smile. Setting my glass down, I glance around the darkened restaurant, which is a small Italian place in a strip mall. It's reputed to have some of the best food in Phoenix, though. It barely holds twenty tables, but they're spaced far enough apart diners feel a measure of privacy. I look back to him, taking the moment to apologize. "I'm sorry about what I said at my house... painting you as something you're not. An elitist."

Aaron shrugs, shooting me a teasing smile. "Maybe I am."

He receives a slow shake of my head. "I don't think so. Truly. At least from what little I've observed so far."

"Well, I appreciate the vote of confidence," he murmurs. "I come from a humble background. I know how fragile the line between fortune and destitution can be."

"How do you know that?" I ask. I don't mean to pry, but he did crack the door.

"Let's just say while growing up, I was in a position where I had a solid, comfortable life, then had it all snatched out from underneath me."

"I'm sorry," I reply, feeling the punch of emotion in his words. But given the fact he started off by saying, "Let's just say…" leads me to believe it's a subject he doesn't want to expound on.

Aaron shrugs again. "I'm just saying I don't take anything about my current fame, wealth, or the ability to pursue a career I'm passionate about for granted. I'm grateful for it every day."

"That is something we definitely have in common. Not the fame or wealth part," I tack on with a laugh. "But I'm really grateful for what I have, too."

Aaron shifts forward in his chair, pushing his empty plate away and placing his forearms on the table. A move that warns an intimate question is forthcoming.

"Why do you distrust fame and fortune? I mean, I get how horrific what that douche did to you was, and I totally get how that would blow your trust in men. But do you blame it on his celebrity, which, in turn, you're projecting on me?"

I wait for a rush of affront, but it doesn't come. Aaron's not belittling my feelings, just trying to understand. Maybe it's because I took the risk in telling him the whole sordid tale that makes it easier for me to accept his curiosity, but I try to explain it as best I can.

I, too, move forward in my chair, mimicking his position with my arms on the table. My arm is perilously close to my plate, which has a bit of red sauce on the edge, but I ignore it. "I'm not sure if it was his own celebrity that made him such an asshole, or maybe it just contributed to it. It's a good question. All I know is I wouldn't have been such a viral joke without his power or fame."

Aaron's eyes search mine, wondering if there's more to it than that. But I think I've boiled it down as best I can about where the source of my mistrust lies.

"You're a conundrum, Clarke Webber," Aaron finally announces, his tone mischievous.

I laugh, nabbing my wineglass for another long sip. Looking over the edge, I ask, "Is that a good or a bad thing?"

"It's an intriguing thing," he admits.

"You know I'm not intentionally trying to be intriguing to get your attention, right?"

"Oh, I know that very well," he murmurs, his tone low and seductive, and makes me wish, just a tiny bit, that I'd shaved my legs.

"I'm going to tell you a secret about me," he says, reaching across the table and removing my glass from my hold. He sets it down, immediately placing his hand over the top of mine.

The touch is so intimate, yet mysterious at the same time, and my breath stalls in my lungs. Still, I manage to whisper, "What's that?"

"I've never done this before," he states boldly, waving around the restaurant with his other hand. "A quiet, romantic dinner. Not a single intention within me other than to have some great conversation with you. No ulterior motives."

This revelation shocks me. It's a vulnerability, really. It's so profound I immediately try to make light of it, merely so he can have an out if he wants it. "Well, it's a good thing I didn't shave my legs, because I came out tonight thinking you might have ulterior motives."

Aaron tips his head back, letting out a laugh that seems to fill the space around us. It's a beautiful sound and I'm mesmerized by his carefree joy at what I just said.

He points a finger. "You see... that right there is

why I'm doing something I wouldn't ordinarily do."

"And what's that?" I ask, curious beyond imagination. Because damn if he isn't just as intriguing.

"I think…" he says thoughtfully, eyes sparkling with challenge and excitement. "I think I'm trying to court you."

CHAPTER 11

Wylde

"THAT'S THE LAST of it," Tacker announces as he pulls one last stick off the back of the trailer, then tosses it onto the pile we'd just unloaded.

"Awesome," I reply, taking off the work gloves he'd given me three hours ago when we started this project. "It sounds like that means it's beer o'clock."

"Definitely," he replies and we both hop into the Gator to head back up to the ranch house.

I'd gladly come out to Shërim Ranch—where Tacker lives with his lady love, Nora—to help with clean up after a storm took down several trees a few months ago. There was simply no time for him to tackle the project during the playoffs, but I'd told him when he was ready to give me a call.

That's what best friends do.

Tacker and I haven't been friends our entire lives, but we're as close to that deep bond as one can get. We first met while playing on the Dallas Mustangs together and through a shared love of working out, badly dubbed martial arts movies, and hockey, we became very close.

That's why it hurt so deeply when he stopped being my friend for a while. But he had reasons.

Good reasons at that.

Tacker went through a loss no man should ever have to endure. He'd been piloting a small aircraft with his fiancée, MJ, aboard and due to an instrument malfunction in bad weather, the plane crashed. MJ died a brutal and slow death in front of him while they were trapped in the wreckage.

Tacker might as well have died in that plane, for the man who returned from that remote slice of land was not the man I'd known. He withdrew from all relationships. Stopped communicating with me, closed himself off to other friends, and generally became a bit of a liability to our hockey team in Dallas. I tried everything—from giving him space to railing at him for letting himself slip away. None of it worked. Nothing mattered to him because he was dead inside.

His saving grace ended up being his transfer to the new expansion team, the Arizona Vengeance. He was traded in the expansion draft, and I'd missed him sorely when he was gone. I'd still tried to maintain contact, but he only sporadically responded. Even when he had, he'd never offered up anything of substance. The few times our teams played against each other, I'd tried to get him to meet up with me after, but he'd declined. While I'd never let him know exactly how deeply that had cut me, I had my own period of grief and mourning over losing my friend in that plane crash.

But everyone has a second chance inside. Fate brought Tacker to the Vengeance team, which ultimately led to him meeting Nora. While I can't go as far as to call her a savior, I will say she's about as close to a saint as one can get by mere virtue of the changes she brought about within him.

Namely... how to forgive himself and move on with his life.

Fate also brought me to the Vengeance, where I'd found my old friend again. While I'm close to many of the men on this team, Tacker is, and always will be, my best friend.

Which is why any day is a good day to hang with him in my book, even if I'm exhausted, sweaty, and covered in scratches.

We ride in companionable silence across rocky terrain toward the main ranch house. Nora actually owns Shërim Ranch, where she specializes in equine therapy. As much as I've enjoyed my reconnection to Tacker, I've equally enjoyed getting to know the woman who brought him back from the brink of disaster. She's warm, funny, kind, and doesn't take any shit from

Tacker. Best of all, she makes him ridiculously happy, which is something I thought I'd never see again.

When we reach the house, we find Nora lounging in a rocking chair. She has her booted feet kicked up on the porch railing, a beer in her hand, and a small cooler at her feet.

As we climb out of the Gator, she says, "Figured you boys would want a cold one."

"I beg of you, Nora," I call out as I round the front and head up the porch steps behind Tacker. "Leave this knucklehead behind and be mine forever."

Nora gives a throaty laugh, but she doesn't respond. She's too busy tipping her head back for the deep kiss Tacker bestows upon her. Ignoring them, I grab a beer from the cooler, plopping down on the porch swing that's perpendicular to the rockers. Tacker takes a seat next to Nora after grabbing his own beer.

Nora holds her bottle up. "Here's to hardworking men."

"Cheers," I reply, holding mine up in salute.

Nora and Tacker tap the necks of their bottles together.

"Want to stay for dinner?" Nora asks. "We're having homemade pizza."

"You better quit feeding him such horrible stuff," I reply slyly, giving him a pointed look. "He'll get fat in the off-season."

"Fuck off," Tacker snarls with good nature. "I can run your puny ass into the ground any day."

Nora ignores our bantering, since she hears it all the time, and adds an extra enticement. "And homemade cheesecake."

"Sounds disgustingly amazing," I reply, sprawling my legs out and starting a slight rock of the swing. "But I've got plans tonight."

"Blonde or brunette?" Tacker teasers.

I ignore the crack. "We're going to an art exhibit downtown."

Both Tacker and Nora stare blankly. I just return a smug smile, then take a casual sip of my beer.

"Did you lose a bet?" Tacker asks.

"Nope."

Tacker pushes out of his rocker, then walks over. He bends at the waist, puts his face close to mine, and tilts his head back and forth as if he's studying me carefully. "I think it's Aaron," he says with a quick glance at Nora. "Looks like him. Smells like him. But it certainly doesn't sound like him."

My fist shoots out, pulling my punch greatly before it hits his stomach, and he makes an exaggerated *oomph* sound while laughing hysterically. He saunters back to his rocker, then lowers his frame into it.

"So you're seriously going on a legit date with a woman to an art exhibit?" Tacker asks, not able to hide his incredulity.

I give him a sour smile. "It's not out of the realm of possibility."

"It's so out of the realm." Tacker chortles. "There's a reason why you're known for your last name... Wylde. You're a love 'em and leave 'em kind of guy. You constantly remind us how mundane we mere mortals who would dare enter into monogamous and committed relationships are."

Nora reaches out, giving Tacker's arm a light smack. "Be nice."

"I am," Tacker insists. "And I'm being truthful."

He'd be right about that. He's calling a spade a spade, and no one knows me better than he does.

"Oh my God," Nora says as if she's just been clued into the answer to a big mystery. "You're talking about Clarke."

"The woman you brought to the weddings?" Tacker asks, surprised. They'd both spent some time talking to her at the two weddings.

"Why is that so shocking?" I grumble.

"Well, because she only went on those dates because she lost a bet," Tacker points out. I'd told him how we'd met. "I thought you were done with her."

"Not quite," I grudgingly admit. "I like her."

Tacker laughs again, delighting in the fact I seem to have been bitten by the same bug he had been struck by.

Same for Bishop, Erik, Legend, and Dax come to think of it. "This is classic," he says with a laugh, then holds his beer up. "Good for you, dude."

"I think it's awesome," Nora praises, as if I need some positive affirmation over my choices. Because if left up to Tacker, he'd probably shame me out of seeing her by convincing me doing so would make me lose some inherent part of myself.

I sip at my beer while Tacker gets control of himself. "So... there's an interesting thing about Clarke."

"What's that?" Nora asks brightly, perhaps cutting off any potential snide remarks from Tacker.

"She had something really humiliating happen to her a few years back," I say hesitantly, not wanting to betray her confidence.

Except it's not exactly a betrayal or a secret, because everyone in the world apparently knows about what happened to her.

Or at least the millions who watched the show and the subsequent masses who used that horrid meme, which I'd googled. It burns me the fuck up, and I can barely look at it anymore.

But I'd really love their advice, and there aren't any others I'd trust more to keep this in confidence.

"So, there was a reality TV show called *Celebrity Proposal*—"

"I know that show," Nora interjects. "I watched it

for a few seasons."

Now I'm the one in shock. I never would have thought she would be into reality TV. But I shake my head and continue. "She was a contestant on the show, and—"

"Oh my God," Nora exclaims in horror, her face immediately morphing into sympathy. "I thought Clarke looked familiar when you first introduced us, but I couldn't place it."

I grimace, realizing Nora knows exactly what I'm talking about. Her expression confirms it was even worse than I suspected.

"That's why I refused to watch that show again," Nora says quietly. "I couldn't stomach what they did to her. The producers really played it up as if she were such a lost cause and someone to be pitied. And then what that guy did—"

"What the fuck are you two talking about?" Tacker growls, feeding into the distress in Nora's tone. He's not laughing anymore. He understands that whatever we're talking about isn't a laughing matter.

Nora turns in her chair to face Tacker, explaining the premise of the show. I can see by the distaste in his expression that he thinks it's as idiotic as I do.

"Anyway," she explains. "Clarke was a contestant, and she made it all the way to near the end."

"Final four," I supply. "And that's when they have

these overnight dates, and she got intimate with the guy."

"Ugh," Nora exclaims in solidarity with Clarke. "That guy was such a dick. A horrible human being."

"What did he do?" Tacker asks.

"After their… um… night together," I continue, my stomach tightening even thinking about Clarke giving up her precious innocence to that freak. "He cut her from the show."

Tacker frowns.

"That's not the bad part," I say. "He went on a drunken video rant afterward about how awful she was. She was a virgin—"

"What in the crazy fuck shit is that?" Tacker snarls. Nora shakes her head in distress, not over his vulgarity, but because she has one of the most tender hearts of anyone I know.

I take a long pull on my beer. "Needless to say, it devastated Clarke. What's worse, they made a meme about her that went viral."

"It was awful," Nora confesses.

"What was the meme?" Tacker asks curiously. I dig out my phone, pull up the screenshot I'd saved when I'd googled it, and hold it out for him to see. He examines it before grimacing and looking away.

I tuck my phone back in my pocket. "Please don't ever let Clarke know I told you about this. I mean, it's not like an unknown, protected secret, but it's so humiliating for her. I just want some advice on how to handle it. She's skittish and mistrustful. I'm not in a rush or anything, but I don't want to scare her off either."

Tacker's mouth parts slightly, his eyes turning a shade warmer. "Dude... you really like her."

"Yeah, I do," I admit, which isn't a hardship to do. I trust Tacker and Nora with my vulnerabilities. Not sure I'd be expressing my feelings to many others, but I know these two are solid.

"And you two are talking about this?" Nora asks, slipping into counseling mode.

"Well, yeah... I mean, she told me all about it and how it made her feel. I pursued her even knowing about it, and I got her to go out with me to dinner last night. I don't know if this will turn into anything, but I do know I still want to see her."

"Seems you're doing everything right if you're talking about it," Tacker says.

"Yes," Nora agrees. "But that was traumatic for her, so there could be triggers."

"That's what I'm afraid of," I admit. "I'm not worried about how I'll treat her. I think I've shown her respect, and I know I'm gaining her trust. But she has it all tangled in her head that the guy's lack of human decency is tied to the fact he was a famous celebrity. Sometimes, she projects that on to me."

"Is she aware of it?" Nora asks.

"Yeah… did it last night, but she immediately caught herself. She apologized."

"That's good," Nora commends, taking a pause to sip her beer. "I guess I'd advise you to also have her toe the line. Seems like she realizes it's not quite fair to judge you based on your own celebrity status. I'd actually advise you not to let her get away with it if she continues to do so."

I nod, accepting her reasoning. It's a delicate balance, I'm guessing, to show her the man I want to be as I continue to explore something with her but doing so without apology for my fame and fortune. It'll be up to me to show her someone can have all that, yet still respect women.

I tip my beer back, finishing it off before pushing out of the swing. "Listen… I appreciate the advice, but I have to get going. Like I said, hot date tonight."

Tacker stands, then walks me to the edge of the porch. Bringing a big hand down on my shoulder, he squeezes. "Look… I didn't mean to give you such a hard time. Got to be honest, this is all shocking, but it also warms my heart. I figured you'd fall one day, and I knew I'd enjoy watching it."

"I haven't fallen yet," I point out, still desiring to maintain a healthy grasp on realism.

"You're definitely tottering, Aaron."

And yeah… I guess I am.

CHAPTER 12

Clarke

WHEN MY DOORBELL rings, I take one last look in my mirror, wondering for the hundredth time if should I ditch the glasses.

Then I decide I'd like to be able to read. I don't feel like dealing with my contacts because I'm so used to my glasses, so Aaron's just going to have to take me as I am.

"Ugh," I mutter, knowing I'm being insane and worrying far too much about the man at my front door.

He asked me to give him the benefit of the doubt, so I'm going to have to put a little trust in that request. It's easier said than done, though, when I worry far too much about maybe ending up hurt.

I spritz on a little bit of DKNY's *Be Delicious* perfume, wondering if the apple fragrance is too immature for a man such as him, but then decide it fits my childish inability to stop worrying about whether he can truly like a woman who wears glasses.

Moving quickly through my house, I glance down to make sure I have shoes on. I do.

White Keds, which I think look cute and sporty with my cuffed-at-the-hem jeans and a blue-and-white striped shirt with three-quarter sleeves. It's going to be a casual evening of visiting an outdoor art exhibit and eating truck food, so I went with super casual.

I swing the door open, preparing for the flutter within me at the first sight of Aaron. He looks far yummier in jeans and a t-shirt than he does dressed up, and our casual attire actually makes me feel more comfortable. I don't like putting on airs and expensive designer finery just isn't who I am.

Aaron's gaze quickly sweeps down my body, then back up, landing on my face with a sly grin. "My apologies for being so bold."

My eyebrows shoot together in confusion. "So bold? What do you mean?"

He shows rather than answers me, hands going to my face to hold me in place as he bends to give me a swift, but sizzling kiss. When he pulls back, my glasses are askew and I have to push them back into place. My eyesight remains a bit blurry, but I suspect it's because the kiss was just that good.

Last night after dinner, he kissed me goodnight at my doorstep. It wasn't a peck on the cheek like the last time, but it was slightly deeper than when he first gave me that surprise kiss at Erik and Blue's wedding. It was enough that I had regretted not shaving my legs, but also left me glad when he walked away because anticipation is half the fun.

"You sure are confident of yourself," I mutter as he steps back.

"Sorry I was so overwhelming." Aaron chuckles, turning to offer his arm. I grab my purse, step out, and lock the door behind me. When I lock my arm into his and he leads me down the porch, he adds, "But you look really great tonight. You look quintessential Clarke."

I glance up as we head for his truck. "What does that even mean?"

"I like you all casual with your hair up in a bouncy ponytail," he replies, his gaze flicking down. "In jeans and sneakers. You appear up for an adventure, and you sort of have this fun vibe about you. I like the way it makes me feel."

His words hit me in a way that actually makes me stumble. He halts our progress, shifting to face me. "You okay?"

I nod, tipping my head back. "It's just... I like you being open with your feelings. That's unusual in most people, much less in men."

Aaron shrugs, guiding me toward his truck again. "Got nothing to be ashamed about, especially not about the way you make me feel."

Another flutter inside my chest, though this one turns into a burning warmth that spreads through me. Aaron just lays it all out there, exactly how he sees it. It touches me on a level that hasn't been touched in, well... forever.

The night only gets better as it progresses, and I think back to what Veronica said about me only dating beta men since the "meme" incident three years ago. I realized I was subconsciously only allowing myself to be with men it wouldn't hurt to walk away from. Men who would never pursue me if I called it quits.

Aaron has relentlessly pursued me from the start. While I realize the risk of getting hurt is greater with a man like him, I also realize I could never be happy with a man who didn't scare me like this. It's that old notion that 'with great risk comes great reward'. It's just been a long time since I've been willing to go out on a limb for it.

We hit the art exhibit, which is set out along the Arizona Canal in downtown Scottsdale, wandering along to examine various mediums and genres. Everything from oil paintings to charcoals, from pottery to sculptures. Aaron takes an interest in a watercolor abstract, which he considers for his condo, but he eventually decides against it because he doesn't trust his own taste. His parting comment as we walk away is,

"Maybe you could check out my living room to give me your opinion about what would look good on the wall."

He says this casually, as if he hopes to have me in his place one day, but like he's not in a rush either. The fact he takes my hand in his, lacing our fingers together, makes me want to melt into him. He has no clue how attractive his nonchalance is, because I understand he's trying to be non-threatening. He's coaxing me out, little by little—leading me toward accepting he is not out to hurt me.

When we get hungry, we hit up a taco truck, because we agree tacos are life. We both get the pork belly with fontina and fresh cilantro, sipping at frosty margaritas in plastic tumblers while sitting at a picnic table.

Aaron's giving me a lesson about hockey—at my request. The more I get to know and like him, the more curious I find myself about what he does for a living. It's hard to reconcile the man I'm getting to know with the professional athlete who plays hockey for a living since I haven't seen him in that capacity because it's the off-season. It doesn't seem real, but it hasn't stopped me from asking questions to try to understand.

Aaron demands a pen out of my purse and on a napkin, he draws a crude replica of a hockey rink, explaining the circles and lines as he goes along.

"Now, when you get called for icing—" he starts,

our heads bent toward each other, but a loud, feminine squeal pierces the air, interrupting us.

"Oh my God," a woman shrieks. "Look... it's Wylde."

I jerk, looking around for the source of the noise, while wondering what "wild" the woman is referencing.

Then we are surrounded... and all I see are bare limbs, deep cleavages, and tanned skin.

It takes me a moment to orient myself, but I soon realize Aaron is being swarmed by a group of what appears to be six or seven women. They're all crowding in close to him, some at his back and sides while one woman leans her hip on the edge of the picnic table, completely blocking my view of him.

To say I'm stunned is an understatement.

So far in the few times we've been out, I've not witnessed Aaron's celebrity status being acknowledged, but now I realize it's because he hasn't truly put himself out in the public. The one date we had at the small Italian restaurant was very private without a lot of people around. No one approached us at all. The two weddings were private affairs as well.

Granted, I've noticed people recognizing Aaron. The times he spent at my bookstore last week, a few customers seemed to know who he was. Most just stared and whispered, but a few asked for pictures and autographs. It was all very low key and respectful with

Aaron being very gracious at the attention.

But this… I don't even know what to think.

The women all start asking for pictures and autographs, a few gushing about how he's their favorite player. I have no clue if they are attending the art exhibit, but, if they are, it's hard to tell. Instead, it appears as if they're dressed to go out clubbing for the evening.

But then the woman perched on the edge of the table scoots back a bit, her curvy ass hitting my margarita and sending it tumbling over. The liquid hits the wooden top, then cascades in a wave right toward me.

Luckily, I'm spry, managing to jump out of my seat before I end up with a lap full of the sticky drink.

And that's when Aaron explodes.

I hadn't even been able to get a good look at him until now with the swarming women blocking my view. But he surges upward from his seat, his face a mask of anger.

"Jesus Christ," he curses viciously, hurrying in a wide arc around the gaggle of females and coming to my side. Taking my wrist in his large hand, he pulls it away from my body and critically studies my clothing. "Did any get on you?"

"I'm fine," I murmur, a tad frightened by his anger, although I understand it's not directed at me.

Aaron turns to glare at the women, who don't even have the grace nor the smarts to appear contrite. Instead, they regard him expectantly, cameras at the ready to pose for pictures with him.

"What is wrong with you?" he demands of the entire group. "I know it was obvious I was enjoying a private moment. Yet, you still swarmed me, pushing your way into our conversation and ruining our meal."

Some of the smiles begin to slide off their perfect, made-up faces. Feeling a tiny bit bad for them, I pull my wrist away from Aaron's grasp, which gets his attention. "It's fine."

"No, it's not," he grits out.

"I don't mind," I assure him. I gesture at the women, who, for the first time, actually seem to see me. A few look downright apologetic. "Why don't you take a few pictures with your fans?"

Aaron stubbornly turns his back on the women, stepping in close and dipping his face to see mine. "I'm really sorry about this."

For the first time since he came into my life, I actually make the first move and touch him. Frowning, I let my hand cup his cheek. "It's fine. Not your fault."

He returns a wry smile. "I know, but it's a blatant reminder of the fame you so desperately hate, which, in turn, is going to make you hate me."

Vigorously, I shake my head. "I don't hate anything

about you, Aaron. I'd never feel that way about you. And I don't hate your fame, either. I understand it's something you have to live with—a part of your everyday reality. It just caught me by surprise, but I'm fine now. I promise."

"It's not usually like that," he assures me. "I think those girls are probably drunk, and they just weren't thinking—"

"It's fine," I say again, meaning it. "And I don't want to piss off your fans, so go take a few pictures, okay?"

"Only if you'll kiss me," he replies, his voice low and rumbling. There's clear yearning in his demand, which, when added to that delicious tone, shoots heat right in between my legs.

"If you insist," I whisper.

Sliding my arms around his neck, I rise on my tiptoes to bring my mouth to his. Tilting my head, I manage to fit against him—my lips touching his and then parting. I let my tongue slip into his mouth, nearly losing all the strength in my legs when he growls in appreciation. His arms band around my waist, hauling me tighter against his hard body, and then Aaron takes over the kiss.

When he finally lets me up for air, I realize he could ask me to do anything right now and I'd say yes.

Regrettably, he only smooths a thumb along my jaw

before taking a step back. With a sigh, he starts to turn to the group of women. Willing to do his duty as a celebrity, he pastes on a welcoming smile.

I lean to the side to peek around him, only to realize the women disappeared. I have no clue when they left, but we are blessedly alone once again.

Aaron grins as he returns his attention my way. "How about another margarita and maybe some dessert?"

"Sounds awesome," I reply, thinking this has turned out to be one of the best dates I've ever been on.

◆

A FEW HOURS later, Aaron walks me to my front door, officially bringing the best date I've ever had to an end. Despite having connected with him on a much deeper level after the earlier fan fiasco, I'm suddenly feeling awkward and unsure of myself.

I fumble in my purse for my keys as we hit my porch, wondering if I should invite him in. Before this date, I did shave, so that barrier has been removed.

Instead, I turn to him and mutter, "I had a great time tonight. Thank you."

Aaron's smile seems sly and a little predatory, which makes my blood start to race. He crowds into my personal space, curling one hand around the nape of my neck while bending to deliver a scorching kiss that wordlessly tells me he had a great time, too, with the additional message that we could have an even better time not so subtly hinted at.

But he pulls his mouth away from mine, moving his lips to my ear to murmur, "I had a great time, too. Call you tomorrow," with absolutely no pressure for more in his tone.

I'm stunned when he starts to turn away from me. Hating my opportunity has passed, I shift toward my door, key in hand.

Then I whip back around. "Would you…"

Aaron pauses, twisting to see me over his shoulder.

"Um… never mind," I whisper. He smiles—his expression conveying understanding, slight amusement, and patience. He gets halfway down the steps before I finally make up my mind and blurt out, "Wait… would you like to come in for a bit?"

Aaron pivots to face me, his head tilted up slightly.

"You know," I prattle on. "We could, um… talk. Or even play Scrabble."

His eyes lock on me, filling with a purpose I don't understand but which causes my tummy to flutter, as Aaron saunters back my way. He takes the porch steps two at a time. Not stopping, he walks right into me. I take a step backward, the door bringing me up short, and Aaron presses in against me, his legs tangling with mine as my breasts mash into his broad chest.

Dipping his head, he puts his mouth near my ear and whispers, "Let's play some Scrabble."

"Okay," I breathe out with a nervous laugh.

Once we're inside, we kick off our shoes. I grab us some waters—Aaron declined alcohol as the two margaritas we had earlier are his limit with driving—and then we settle in cross-legged on my living room floor with the game board between us.

We chat easily through the first game, which I win. As we're setting up for the second, Aaron asks, "How often do you see your parents?"

He knows my parents live near here and they're both accountants who dabble in rental properties as a means of securing an earlier retirement.

I shrug. "Not as often as I'd like. The store takes up most of my time. Sunday is my only real day off."

"You work too hard," Aaron observes.

"So says the guy who will be working virtually seven days a week during hockey season between travel, games, and practice." I'd learned a lot tonight when he'd explained all about his career.

"Touché..." He smirks, laying out his tiles to spell the first word of this game—B-E-N-C-H. He tallies up the points, then writes them down before looking up. "Why don't you hire more help?"

"If I did that, I'd go under," I say truthfully. "My passion isn't a great moneymaker. I make just enough to pay my bills, sock a little away in retirement, and put some decent groceries on the table."

Aaron blinks, and I wonder if he's disappointed the woman he probably thought was a savvy businesswoman is barely hanging on. Instead, his smile turns warm and he says, "I admire that. Working hard for what you love instead of how much you can make."

His praise warms me, fulfilling my base need for someone to acknowledge that what I'm doing has purpose. My parents think it's a pipe dream, and they've only been vaguely encouraging. Not because they don't love me, but because they want better for me.

"My parents—who I swear love me dearly—are constantly suggesting I move on to something a little more stable in the money department," I say. "It's times like those when I wish I had a sibling to take some of their attention off my shortcomings."

"Not shortcomings," he corrects sternly while I muse over my tiles. "Grand ambitions."

I grin as I choose my word. "I like that. Thanks."

I place my tiles, using the C in his word to spell out C-A-R-T-E-L. After I calculate my points, I add them to the list.

"What about you?" I ask teasingly. "Do you have any siblings you overshadow with your greatness?"

Aaron chuckles, but his answer is decidedly vague. "I have a half-sister I'm not overly close to. But she's definitely the apple of her parents' eyes."

That statement makes me sad, because maybe there's still a little bit of romanticism left within me. I feel like everyone should be close to their siblings. Not that I would know, but there have been many times I'd pined for one while growing up.

It's not something I feel I can press him on, so I voluntarily change the subject. "When will you get your day with the Cup?" I ask.

Aaron's eyes lift to mine, and he smiles. He loves hockey, and he lights up whenever we talk about it. That's okay, because I feel the same type of joy when I talk about my bookstore. "Maybe in a few weeks. I was going to have a party at my condo. Nothing big. I hope you'll come."

"I'd love to," I say, and it makes me a bit giddy to think Aaron and I are planning out time together a few weeks from now. "I can't even imagine how incredible it was to win that championship."

I had done some reading up on the Vengeance and their journey to win the Cup this year. It's a bit of a sports miracle.

Aaron places a palm on the floor to brace himself, his face warming at the nostalgic memory I'm placing before him. "The feeling of that win... there's nothing like it. I'd go so far as to say it's the best feeling I've ever had."

Aaron spells out the word R-A-T, and I snicker as he calculates his measly points.

"What's one thing you would change about yourself if you could?" he asks as he picks out his new tiles.

It's a deep question. I study him thoughtfully until his gaze rises to meet mine. He shrugs. "I'm just curious because I think you're practically perfect. But, admittedly, I don't know you all that well. Just trying to speed up the process."

Okay, now that's adorable. When coupled with the fact the man came into my house to play Scrabble with me because he knows how nervous I am and that I'm not sure what in the hell I'm doing, and I'm afraid my heart is starting to take a bit of a tumble for him.

I look at the ceiling, pondering his question. When I return my attention to him, I say, "I wish I could be more spontaneous. Not have to overthink or plan out everything."

Aaron's lips curve up, his eyes warm with understanding. It's obvious he appreciates the truthfulness of my answer. He leans forward across the Scrabble board.

We meet in the middle for a soft, sweetly tender kiss that says nothing more than, "Hello again... I think I really like you."

It almost seems too romantic to be true.

But then his tongue touches mine, and the kiss takes a deeper turn. Before I know it, we're both on our knees and are making out like two fevered teenage kids. My breasts are mashed into his chest, and both his hands are in my hair to hold me still so he can ravage my mouth. Our breathing turns heavy, and I have the strange desire to rip all of his clothes off so I can touch every inch of his body.

Aaron tears his mouth from mine, and even though he still holds my head, he leans back so he can look me in the eye. His chest is still heaving, as is mine.

His smile is regretful and amused all at the same time. "We should slow down."

My brows knit together, and the minute he sees my confusion, he leans into me for a quick but tender kiss. "We can take our time, Clarke. It's actually kind of refreshing, to be honest…"

I can't help myself. If there's something else I wish I could change, it's the insecurity that comes from having been publicly called a terrible lay. It makes me doubt myself.

Aaron is beyond perceptive, though. Whatever my expression is revealing of my inner thoughts, he latches on to them and starts vehemently shaking his head. "Oh no you don't," he orders in a commanding growl. "Don't you even start thinking I don't want you."

Well, damn… that's exactly what I was thinking.

To my shock, Aaron's fingers band around my wrist, then he starts to drag my hand right down to the bulge straining against his jeans. My eyes widen as I take it in just a mere second before he presses my palm to it.

And it's huge. Massive. Causes excitement to start pulsing between my legs, but I'm distracted by his low baritone voice, which causes my eyes to lift and lock with his. "Don't ever have any doubt about how much I desire you, Clarke. But I want you to be with me all the way. I want you to entirely trust me, and not just get carried away by physical lust."

We stare at each other, faces mere inches apart, and my hand pressed firmly against his erection. All I can do is nod my understanding because my throat is absolutely parched right now.

"How about dinner tomorrow night?" he murmurs, leaning in to graze his lips softly across mine at the same time he releases his hold on my wrist. "I found this great Greek place last month."

"How about I cook for you?" I suggest instead.

Aaron pulls back, regarding me with deep contemplation. What is that going to look like... tomorrow... him back in my house for a home-cooked meal?

He grins. "Now see... that's spontaneous."

I can't help but laugh. My palms going to his chest, I lean forward to rest my forehead there for just a moment. I feel Aaron's lips press to the back of my head, and I realize even if he doesn't feel it... I trust him.

CHAPTER 13

Wylde

"**A**ND THAT'S THE last of it," Baden says as he puts an empty cooler in the back of my truck before closing the tailgate.

"Want to grab some lunch?" I ask him and Kane, the latter eating a small bag of Doritos as we stand around the rear of my truck.

Kane holds the bag up. "This sure isn't going to tide me over until dinner."

"I stole a sandwich while in there," Baden says, thumbing over his shoulder at the building we'd just left. "Well, I didn't steal it. One of the volunteers thought I looked hungry, and they pressed it into my hand."

Baden, Kane, and I just got done passing out over one thousand meals to the homeless in that building. It's one of the many Phoenix-area homeless shelters we're working with in conjunction with the Vengeance organization to help combat the growing issue. We'd met with the entire team and assorted family members at the arena where truckloads of donated food arrived today. We worked on assembly lines, making sandwiches and vats of soup as well as snack bags. After, we'd loaded up in individual vehicles in small teams of two or three to hit the various shelters around town. We handled the lunch rush for this particular shelter, and it killed me to see so many children in line waiting for what would be their only meal today. It had a profound effect on Kane and Baden as well.

As we were loading up the empty coolers, we all agreed we'd like to do more, but we're just not sure what more we can do at this point. Definitely a conversation we can continue over lunch.

I nod toward the truck and we get in, Kane taking the front seat and Baden getting into the back of the extended cab.

"Mind if we make a quick stop along the way?" I ask.

They both mutter their assent. I figure I can't be this close to Clarke's store without stopping in to say a quick hello.

Sure, I just saw her last night where that kiss had me about ready to fuck her right there on top of the Scrabble board, and, yes, I'm going to see her for dinner this evening, but I can't seem to fucking help myself. I'd like to see her in the middle of the day, too.

We're no more than five blocks from her shop and while there's not a parallel spot right in front, I find one half-a-block down. After I feed the meter, the guys get out of the truck to follow me.

It's Baden who finally asks, "Where are we going?"

Kane makes the accurate guess. "To see his girl-friend."

Baden, of course, is stunned and it takes me no more than the half-block we have to walk to fill him in on the fact I'm still seeing the beautiful redhead I'd brought to the weddings.

Just as we're about to enter, my phone rings. I recognize the number, but it's a call I don't have time to take at the moment. I hit the button that will send it to voice mail, intent on returning the call as soon as I leave Clarke's store.

The bells announce our arrival, and I see Veronica behind the register helping a customer. This doesn't surprise me as Clarke told me her friend often helps out around the place. She apparently does this for free, because Clarke also told me that Veronica received so much money in her divorce settlement she never has to work another day in her life if she doesn't want to. The only problem is that Veronica is incredibly bored being a rich divorcee, so she works here more often than not while she tries to figure out what to do with her life.

She shoots me a welcoming smile. Clarke had introduced us during one of my forays into the store. Just last week, she was polite but regarded me with a bit of skepticism.

Not sure what Clarke has told her since our last few days together, but Veronica's smile is definitely warmer.

Which is nice but not a requirement.

Baden and Kane walk in behind me, Baden mumbling the word "damn" in an appreciative way under his breath. That means he laid eyes on Veronica, who is every bit of the knockout she has made herself up to be. She's wearing a wraparound dress that does wonders for her body, and her face is flawlessly beautiful.

I barely spare her a thought as I start walking along the rows of shelves in search of Clarke.

I find her in the third row, a box on the floor at her feet as she slides books into their appropriate spots.

My movement catches her eye. I have to say the delight on her face when she sees me feels pretty fucking good. I've never had anyone look at me quite that way before.

Sure, I've had women regard me appreciatively, but that has to do with either my physical attributes or the celebrity that comes attached to my name.

Clarke appears as if I just turned her day from good to insanely fucking awesome.

"Hey… what are you doing here?" she asks, brushing a lock of hair back from the corner of her glasses.

"In the area, so I just thought I'd drop in," I reply as I walk toward her. I don't hesitate because I don't know how long we'll have this cherished bit of privacy, but I lean in and give her a long, slow kiss. She fucking purrs as she melts into me, and I have to end our embrace before my body reacts.

When I hear Veronica laugh, I figure Kane or Baden must be entertaining her. I take Clarke's hand, then lead her to the front of the store.

The men turn to us as we approach, and I take a moment for re-introductions. They had met briefly at Erik and Blue's wedding, but, this time, with my hand at her lower back, it's clear we're much more than just a one-off wedding date.

"What were you guys up to today?" Clarke asks.

I tell her about the food drive to feed the homeless at various shelters today, and yeah... I like the way her eyes warm at the knowledge and how it obviously endears me to her even more. Anything I can do to keep building up that trust so she can forget about the vile shit that douchebag did to her and realize not all guys are the same.

"In fact," I continue. "We were just on our way to grab some lunch. Want to come with us?"

Clarke shakes her head regrettably. "I'd love to, but it's just not possible."

I look pointedly over at Veronica. "And yet, I bet Veronica wouldn't mind you leaving for a bit."

As if taking some pre-agreed-upon cue, Veronica nods a little too exuberantly. "She'd love to go with you. I can totally watch the store."

Clarke cuts Veronica a chastising scowl. "Have you forgotten I asked you to come in to help me get the stocking done so I could leave early to cook for this big lout," and here she slaps her hand into my stomach, "a nice meal?"

That she made the effort to handle her duties so she could leave work early touches me.

She did that for me.

Veronica laughs as she shrugs, shooting me a look that says, "I tried".

Clarke reaches down, laces her fingers with mine, and gives me a squeeze. "I'd really love to, but I do want to get out early to hit the grocery store, and, well... I just want some extra time before you come over to make things perfect."

She blushes the minute the words tumble out of her mouth, her gaze cutting over to Kane, Baden, and Veronica as she realizes she said something sweet with a little bit of innuendo laced in, and she did so in front of an audience.

"I just mean," she blurts out, "that the dish I'm planning to make is complicated. It takes time, and I don't want to be rushed."

Chuckling, I lean over and put my mouth near her ear, whispering for her benefit and no other. "I cannot wait for you to feed me tonight."

She blushes prettily, because while the words were innocent in and of themselves, the low rumble by which I delivered them so privately to her spoke of other things that might not be.

I bestow a kiss on the corner of her mouth and pull away, turning toward my friends. "You guys ready to go?"

Kane and Baden bid farewell to Veronica and I wonder if either might be hitting me up later for more info about her. While she is indeed beautiful and incredibly single, the one thing I noticed in the small interaction between Veronica and the guys is she hadn't overtly flirted with either.

"Oh, Aaron... wait," Clarke calls, causing me to stop and twist back toward her.

Kane snickers. "Aaron? No one calls him Aaron."

I shove an elbow backward, catching him in the ribs. I haven't had to explain to Clarke that most people call me Wylde because it was me living up to my reputation with the women.

Clarke moves behind the counter, bends to grab something, then comes back around toward me with a book in her hand.

I look down as she hands it over, proclaiming. "*Harry Potter and the Chamber of Secrets.*"

I grin, taking it from her. Holding up the paperback, I examine the illustration. "Awesome."

"You're kidding, right?" Kane asks with a laugh.

Shooting him a glare, I reach into my back pocket for my wallet to fish out some cash for the book. When Clarke's hand comes down on my wrist, my attention goes back to her.

She shakes her head. "My gift to you."

I've never had a woman give me anything before, and the fact it's from Clarke and there's probably nothing more personal she could give me than a book hits me deep.

I drop a hand on the nape of her neck, then press a long kiss to her mouth, bending her slightly backward while doing so.

Baden gives an uncomfortable-sounding cough, and Veronica says, "Just so you two know... guys who read are hot."

"Really?" Kane asks curiously.

"Really," she affirms.

I let Clarke up from my kiss, watching her eyes flutter open. She gives me a dopey smile, and I like that I dazed her. She does the same to me at times.

"See you tonight," I murmur.

Kane and Baden follow me out onto the sidewalk,

discussing what books they've read and whether women would find it sexy. I ignore them, pulling my phone out and returning the call I got right before I walked into Clarke's store.

He answers on the second ring. "Walt Nichols."

"It's Aaron Wylde," I say into the receiver, although I'm sure he already knows from caller ID.

"Mr. Wylde... I got the information you asked for."

I listen to the man as we walk back to my truck, Baden and Kane following just one pace behind me. By the time I'm unlocking my vehicle, I've heard enough to give me several ideas.

"Can you send everything to my email?" I ask Walt, the private investigator I'd hired to look into Tripp Horschen, the man who destroyed Clarke's heart and confidence.

"Sure thing," he replies before disconnecting.

I pull my keys out of my pocket, looking across the bed of my truck to Kane and Baden. "Let me ask you guys something."

"What's up?" Baden replies.

"If someone hurt a person you cared about—not physically, but mentally and emotionally—would you do something about it?"

"Without a doubt," Kane responds even as Baden nods his agreement.

"How far would you go?" I ask, calculating my options.

Kane leans his arms on top of my truck bed, narrowing his gaze on me. "I wouldn't do anything that would put my career in jeopardy."

"So kicking his ass is out of the question?" I posit.

"Can you hurt him in other ways?" Baden asks, all of this being hypothetical thoughts among friends.

"Seems like I can," I reply, eager to see the stuff Walt Nichols promised to send me.

Baden and Kane shoot each other knowing looks, because they know me. Know once I set my sights on something, I don't give up until my mission is accomplished.

They'd have to be idiots not to understand I'm talking about something that happened to Clarke. They just had a seat, front row and center, to the slightly foolish and punch-drunk way I act around her.

Still, they don't ask for details, which I appreciate, because I'd never share with them what happened to her. I might have revealed it to Tacker and Nora, but he's my best friend and she's a licensed therapist. Their advice was gold.

I don't need advice now, though.

No matter what the future holds for Clarke and me, the one thing I'm most certain of is I'm going to make Tripp Horschen pay tenfold for what he did to her.

CHAPTER 14

Clarke

ARON HELPS ME out of his truck, which has become a natural event between us. We've been out every single night this week and outside of the one time I cooked him dinner three nights ago, we've gone out to different restaurants.

I have to say, I'm getting a little bit better about handling his fame. We haven't had another incident like that night where the women swarmed him. In hindsight, I think that had to do more with the amount of alcohol they had imbibed.

But I'm finding the more time we spend out in public, the more often he's recognized as a Vengeance player. Most of the time, people don't even approach him, but I do see them pull out cameras to take pictures or videos. Those who do approach, for the most part, are polite and well aware they are intruding. There was only one occasion when a man interrupted us at dinner, and that was just this evening.

Aaron had chosen another small, out-of-the-way restaurant and even made the reservation requesting a private table near the back. The restaurant was dimly lit with flickering candles and soft music—definitely for the romantics. The man himself was there with a woman, whom he left at their table to approach us while we were just starting the main course. I held my breath, wondering what Aaron would do.

He was pissed at those women and hadn't minded letting them know it. Later, he'd told me it was the one girl knocking over my drink that had tipped him over the edge.

But tonight, Aaron obliged the man, although I could tell he wasn't overly happy about it. He indulged the fan's request for an autograph and a photograph, but when the man tried to start talking hockey with him, Aaron had merely held up a hand. The guy's mouth had snapped shut, his gaze settling on me when Aaron nodded my way and said, "Look... I'm out for a nice dinner with this amazingly beautiful woman, so I'd appreciate it if you could respect our privacy now."

The man was profusely apologetic as he backed away. I watched as he returned to his table, the woman he'd been with lit into him, and it was clear the tongue lashing he got would make an impression. He'd looked pretty hang-dogged after that.

But now, Aaron walks me to my door as he has the past two nights. He has been so low pressure I've been wondering if I've read him wrong. Maybe he only wants friendship, or maybe he's being so cautious with me because he's waiting on me to give him a sign.

All I really know for sure is I've been thinking about having sex with him way too much. Like I'm obsessing about it, to be honest.

I pull my keys out of my purse, preparing to invite Aaron in as I usually do. The night before last he accepted, and he came in to watch a movie with me. I'd ended up falling asleep on his shoulder.

Last night, he'd declined, stating he had an early workout planned with Tacker.

Before I can get the invitation out, though, Aaron takes my face in his hands—and I love so much when he does that because it puts me completely under his control—and presses his mouth to mine. As usually happens when this man kisses me, my circuits fry and go haywire. I have a hard time thinking, all rational thought melting into a puddle of goo. As always, my hands go around his neck to hang on as I simply kiss him back.

This is different. Usually, when we start to make out, it's right before our evening is concluding and he knows he's only going to let it go so far before he puts a stop to it. We've been getting bolder and bolder in our touches at night, and I know he leaves in some physical discomfort.

But Aaron initiates this kiss before we've even decided whether our date is over or will continue inside. The prospect that maybe he's done waiting excites me, and I press in closer.

He moves a hand to the back of my head, grips a handful of hair, and slides his mouth to my neck. I shiver at the touch, his lips so damn skillful the barest touch causes a cascading ripple effect throughout me.

"Do you want to come in?" I gasp as his teeth scrape along the muscle running along the side of my neck.

His tone is low, soft, and barely audible. "You know if I come inside tonight, I'm going to take my shot at getting in your panties, right? I'm tired of wondering if my kisses make you wet."

Oh, God.

Oh. My. God.

My legs turn rubbery. I've never heard Aaron be this direct before. He's always been such a gentleman, keeping our conversations light and easy. He makes me laugh, and now he has me wanting to weep with desire. His dirty talk is so shocking I freeze with inaction. I have no clue how to even respond to that, except my body is demanding I accept his challenge. I can feel it right between my legs, the fact my panties are indeed damp right now is a testament.

All I can do is nod my understanding of the situation. It's my tacit permission saying I'm more than willing for him to take that shot.

I take a deep breath and as I let it out, I turn from him to unlock my door. My mind races as I insert the key. Did I make my bed this morning? Are the sheets fresh? Should I excuse myself to brush my teeth first?

I open the door, then step across the threshold. Should I offer to open a bottle of wine? Do I bring out the Scrabble board?

No, wait... that's horrible foreplay. Scrabble? Christ, you're a damn dork, Clarke.

And oh my God... does he have condoms? Because I don't...

Surely he does.

Think, Clarke. Think.

Okay, let's start with wine... a glass to help me relax.

I turn to face Aaron, who's shutting the door behind him. When I open my mouth to ask if he prefers red or white, he immediately fills it with his tongue.

Aaron is on me, inside of me. His hands hold tight to my waist as he turns me... backs me into the wall... and pins me there with the deepest, sexiest, most spine-tingling kiss I've ever received in my life. My fingers clutch his shirt, tightening and twisting the cotton between my claws for sheer leverage as I try to kiss him back with my best moves.

A low rumble sounds in his chest, then his mouth is on my neck, kissing down to my shoulder. His hands go around my back to slide under my shirt and stroke my skin.

Aaron's mouth is magic, moving from my neck to my mouth. His tongue enthralls me, making me a slave.

My pulse hammers as he completely overwhelms me. Right here in my living room, pressed against the wall.

Somehow, his hands find their way to my lower back, then around to my hips where his skillful hands start to pull up the simple cotton skirt I'm wearing. Cool air hits my thighs, then Aaron's palm is pressed right to my core.

I gasp, my hips shooting forward, and I can't help the tiny grinding motion I make. Aaron laughs darkly at my response. With his breath on my neck causing shivers, his finger works under the elastic of my panties and strokes through my wet folds.

"Oh God," I moan, my head falling back and thunking hard against the wall.

A long, thick finger slides into me and my muscles contract hard around him, gripping and sucking him in deeper.

"Christ, Clarke," he mutters through gritted teeth. "So responsive, baby."

He has no clue. I've never felt anything like this before, and I haven't the foggiest idea why. He's not the first man I've passionately made out with, nor the first to finger me.

I suspect it has something to do with the total package that is simply Aaron Wylde. The player who usually never gives the same woman his attention twice. The man who has listened to my darkest, most humiliating secret, and validated my feelings. The celebrity who is as down to earth as I could ever imagine someone famous to be.

And finally, the guy who has taken his time to make me so ready for this moment that I'm ready to climb him like a tree so I can ride his hand.

"More," I manage to squeak out in a plaintive request or through harsh wheezing. I'm not sure which, but it didn't sound pretty.

I get another dark laugh from Aaron, then another finger. His mouth ravages me again in a kiss so deep I can only hang on while letting him do his worst.

It's when his thumb comes into play, alternately strumming my clit between the deep pump of his fingers inside me, that I start to get a little crazy.

"Aaron," I moan, turning my face away from his kiss. "Please… I need you inside me."

"Not even close to getting there, Clarke," he mutters, his hand gripping my hair and holding my head still so he can claim my lips again.

Not even close? How can he say that? My body is ready. I have barely touched him, yet I can feel his thick erection intermittently pressing into my belly as my lower half wiggles and squirms around his hand between my legs.

It's usually at this point when a man gets me worked up that I beg for him to get inside me... and he obliges.

Aaron doesn't seem to be in any rush at all, though, and it makes me realize he's definitely different from anyone I've ever been with. He's not into instant gratification, and there's something so alpha, so *sexy*, about that I can feel my orgasm starting to brew just from the revelation.

Well, because of what his fingers and thumb are doing, too, but still... the knowledge Aaron is so strong, capable, and in control manipulates my body just as much as his actions.

I cry out when Aaron stretches me with a third finger, pushing them in deep and when he pulls them out, it's to concentrate all that wetness he just pulled from me right at my clit. His fingers rub and flick and pinch. He flutters them quickly, exerting just enough pressure to keep my orgasm elusive, which forces me into a much more willing participant to torture than I care to be.

Now I'm practically humping his hand while gripping onto his shoulders. Aaron pulls back from me, giving me a respite long enough to look down in between our bodies. I watch his face darken, filling with a feral appreciation of how wild he's driving me, then he growls, "That's it, Clarke. Show me how much you want it."

God, I want it so bad. There's a slight flash of shame when I finally beg, "Please, Aaron, let me come."

Aaron's eyes snap to mine and whatever he sees on my face reflects back on his as sheer determination and focus. His head dips, his mouth covering mine as his fingers attack my clit. There's no soft-as-petal caresses now—he all-out ravages me, right between my legs.

The force of my orgasm catches me so unaware I shriek when I come, and it sounds as if I'm in pain.

But I'm not.

I'm free and breaking apart so fabulously, so much harder than I ever have before. The world could end right now, and I'd go happily into the oblivion.

"Room?" Aaron grunts and while I hear the word clearly, I don't understand it at all.

"Room?" I repeat dully, my body still spasming with ripples of pleasure as his finger lazily strokes me.

"Your bedroom," he clarifies.

"Oh," I reply with a dreamy smile. "Down the hall, last door on the right."

And then I'm in Aaron's arms, him having swept me

up in a purely romantic fashion. I don't even have time to be embarrassed my skirt is around my waist, or to care his shoulder careens off the corner wall where my living room meets the hallway, or how he fumbles with the light switch at the door until he ends up flooding the entire room with too-bright light from my overhead fixture.

Aaron carries me to my bed—to the end—and actually drops me there like a bag of bricks. I don't have time to be surprised or even offended by his rough treatment because his hands are immediately all over me.

My sandals come off, then go flying over his shoulder. His fingers slip into the elastic waistband of my skirt, managing to hook my panties at the same time, and he yanks them down my legs.

Immediately, I'm embarrassingly aware of being half-naked and splayed out under a bright light. I slide my hands down my belly to cover my crotch, but I stop when Aaron's eyebrows shoot together, and he gives me a fierce glare. "Don't even think about covering yourself."

"Turn out the light then," I snap, keeping my fingers hovering over my stomach.

"Not a chance," he says with a leer. "I've been dreaming of this moment for two weeks, and I'm not missing a single scintillating moment of your gorgeous body. So keep your hands away from down there unless you want to play with yourself—"

"Aaron," I exclaim, feeling the burn of embarrassment engulf my ears.

With another lecherous grin, he shakes his head. "I've got so many things to show you, Clarke."

I can feel my blush spreading over my entire body, but I don't have time to be self-conscious about it. Aaron extends his meaty fist, grabs a hunk of my shirt, and lifts my torso off the bed until I'm sitting, my lower half completely naked and legs splayed out in front of me.

He bends to place a soft kiss on my mouth, then, ever so gently, he removes my glasses. I almost fall backward when he releases his grip on my clothing, but he only turns to the dresser behind him to set my glasses down. When he shifts back my way, his expression is focused as he takes one long stride to reach the bed again.

His hands come out and before I even understand what's happening, my shirt and bra are off and being tossed to the floor.

Aaron takes a half step back, raking his eyes over me. I've never felt more foolish in my life as I sit upright with my legs straight out, which doesn't flatter my stomach in the least. My gaze falters, falling away from his burning one.

"You're beautiful, Clarke," Aaron murmurs and despite my extreme discomfort in the bright light of my room, I can't help but look up.

I expect him to talk me down from my horrible lack of self-confidence between the sheets so to speak, the residual damage left over from the horrible experience losing my virginity saddled me with.

Instead, my mouth goes desert dry when Aaron merely lifts his t-shirt over his head. He does it slowly, revealing inch after inch of smooth, tanned skin and rippling muscles. His broad chest and strong shoulders corded with muscles are revealed, the shirt falling from his fingers to the floor.

"Let's get on equal footing, okay?" he asks gently.

I can only nod.

Aaron toes off his shoes, then sits beside me on the bed to remove his socks. When he stands, he pulls his belt off slowly but with assurance. His jeans and underwear come off next in the same move. Overwhelmed, I stare at the beauty of his body as it's revealed.

Sadly, I realize I've never taken a really good look at any of the men I've been with in the past. Lights had usually been off. Sometimes, it had just been drunken fumbling. Other times, the act had been performed so hastily that not all clothing had come off.

And those instances had been fine. Adequately enjoyable. Although the thought of Aaron and me hastily going at each other without the patience to fully undress has huge appeal... at a future date and with the knowledge the result would be way hotter than any of those fumbling experiences.

But in this moment, Aaron clearly wants me to examine his body. He wants me to enjoy each inch he reveals.

He's wordlessly telling me—as he stands before me like a golden Adonis all muscled and with his thick, long shaft fully engaged—that I have every right to gaze at him until my heart is content.

He's so beautiful. I'm not quite sure my heart will ever be content, but I don't feel foolish at all right now.

I feel hot and needy. I want to not only see him, but also feel him as well.

Aaron's expression softens as he watches my body visibly start to relax. He steps closer to the bed, his tall frame bringing that big damn cock my way. It's going to be tough for my body to take him... but take him I will.

Aaron's warm hand presses to the center of my chest, pushing me down onto my mattress. I expect him to climb right on top, commencing with round two of making out, as skilled as the man is at kissing.

Instead, I give a sharp yelp when he grabs my ankles and drags me to the edge of the mattress until my butt almost hangs off the edge.

"What—" I start to ask, but the words clog in my throat when Aaron drops to his knees. He bends forward, his warm breath caressing my lower stomach and the insides of my thighs.

My mind flashes with a moment of clarity, instinctively knowing what he is about to do, and I involuntarily try to close my legs. No man has ever done *that* to me before, and I'm as terrified as I am excited by the prospect.

"Keep 'em spread," Aaron orders gruffly, the only warning I get before his mouth descends onto my most private place.

Suddenly, I'm pretty sure I'm going to come out on the other side of this as a completely changed woman.

CHAPTER 15

Wylde

GODDAMN IT, SHE tastes amazing, but... I knew she would. Just knew it down to the depths of my tingling balls, which are aching with the need to be inside her.

But there is no way I'm fucking Clarke until I make her come at least one more time. Yes, that has everything to do with my own male ego.

Having the knowledge about how horrible her first experience was—knowing the dickhead who took her virginity didn't do a damn thing to make it good for her—well, I'm going to rock her fucking world so hard she's going to be ruined for any other man for the rest of her life. And I don't even feel bad about it.

Her sex is warm and soft. The skin under my hands is silky soft when I slip my arms under her legs, curl them past her hips, and bring my fingertips over the top of her pelvis to open her pussy wide for me.

"Aaron," Clarke cries out at the first touch of my tongue to her clit, garbled pleas for me to *stop... oh God, don't stop... please stop, God... don't stop...* Hard to be sure which going by her contradicting demands, and it makes me chuckle.

Never going to stop—and she doesn't actually want me to—so her confliction doesn't bother me.

My goal is to decimate her senses—so far, so good. Luckily, my mouth is one of the best weapons I have. I fucking love kissing a woman. Could spend hours doing it. I look forward to spending some time with Clarke, maybe just slowly making out on her couch one night.

That's not going to happen until I get my fill of her, though, and I'm not sure how many times or weeks that may end up taking.

Plunging my tongue deep inside her, I pull it out and lash at her most sensitive part. Clarke screams, begs, and bucks wildly underneath me.

The bucking part turns me on. I like the thought of Clarke believing she has any control over this, because it'll be so hot when she realizes she doesn't. Of course, all she ever has to do is say the word "no" and I'll stop, but while all systems are on an agreed full-speed-ahead course, her cries and begging only add fuel to the fire. Only encourage me even more—urging me to make her come harder, more explosively, than the first time.

I eat at Clarke like a starved man who has never had

such delicious-tasting sustenance. Inhaling her sweet muskiness with pure desire tickling my nose, I could happily keep my face buried between her legs for days on end.

Clarke continues to buck and cry out. Fingers twining in my hair, she jerks hard, desperate for something she has no control over receiving. That's all up to me.

I sense her getting close, so I gentle my tongue, lapping her like a bowl of cream. When she seems to start to calm down, I roughly lash my tongue over her— quick strokes designed to build her fire back up again.

"Please, God... Aaron... please," she whimpers, almost a wail, her head thrashing from side to side. At that moment, I smile against her pussy because she fucking belongs to me one hundred percent now.

Pressing my tongue to her, I flutter it quickly across the over-sensitized engorgement that holds the secret to her satisfaction. For a heartbeat, Clarke goes utterly still, her eyes squeezed tightly shut as if she's concentrating... and then she explodes underneath me. Her entire body arches off the bed, bowing so deeply I'm afraid her spine will crack. She doesn't scream or cry out, but rather utters a deep groan that sounds like the earth rumbling before a quake finally wrenches it apart.

And then she shocks me by uttering the word "*fuck*" over and over in a long, staccato burst of release. It's not that Clarke doesn't curse, but I haven't heard her lob the filthiest of all words before, so it's sexy as hell coming from her at this moment.

She flops back down to the bed, gasping for air and I take a moment as I push up from my kneeling position to note with satisfaction her entire body is still trembling. I want to watch her try to pull herself back together, but I've got more pressing needs.

Namely, my aching dick, which is incredibly pissed at being ignored for so long. Lurching around, I bend and grab my jeans.

My wallet.

Then the condom inside. It's one of three I stashed in there a few weeks ago—before our first wedding date. I had originally thought I'd have already had to replace them by now, but, honestly, I'm glad they've remained sealed.

This is way better than anything I ever thought I'd have with Clarke.

Clarke mutters something under her breath and lifts her head from the bed, staring at me with fuzzy eyes and pink cheeks. Her nipples are pebbled, most likely from the orgasm she just had, and I make a mental note to give them some attention.

After making quick work of the condom wrapper, I fist myself and roll the rubber on. Clarke's eyes widen as she watches, her mouth parting slightly as her little pink tongue flicks out to swipe her lip. I have to work hard to hold back my groan, even more so to control myself so I don't pounce on her.

It's not going to be easy.

Not with the way she's gazing at me.

At my cock, actually, which seems to pound with an aching need to get inside her.

I drag in a shaky breath, calling on some goddamn self-control. Angry at myself, as well as slightly amused since I've never been so out of sorts with a woman before, I raise one leg and press my knee into the mattress on the outside of Clarke's bare thigh.

She instinctively scrambles backward up the mattress, but not in an effort to escape.

Merely to accommodate.

My other leg comes up, too. By some means, she and I meet exactly in the middle of the bed. Clarke's hazel eyes somehow glow even greener—her desire, perhaps? Her legs spread, causing the outsides of her thighs to nudge against the insides of mine, and I shift until I'm perfectly nestled in between her legs.

Exactly where I need to be.

Elbows pressed into the mattress to hold my weight off her, I dip my head and bring my mouth not to hers, but to her nipple instead. I kiss it softly, touching the tip of my tongue to it and relishing her appreciative moan as her fingers slide into the softness of my hair.

My hips lower slightly, the length of my cock pressing onto her pelvis. Clarke gyrates her hips, a move that doesn't go easy on my aching shaft, and I nibble sharply at her nipple with my teeth. The cutest, most unladylike grunt erupts from her as her legs slide outward, creating more of an invitation. She slides a hand to my ass, trying to urge me even closer.

Trying to get me inside of her.

But first, I have to do one more thing. I need her mouth again, because I have found such supreme beauty in kissing it. I also want her to taste herself on my lips— to know there won't be any barriers between us in this bed. Just as one day, I expect her to kiss me after she's taken me deep inside her throat, so we can share everything.

I snort, not able to hide the tiny bark of laughter at my internal musings. I've turned into a fucking poet because of the woman beneath me.

Clarke's eyes fill with curiosity, probably wondering about the slight curve to my mouth, but I merely touch my lips to hers. Eagerly, she opens for me. As my tongue slides in against hers, I take my cock in hand and find the exact place I must possess. When I deepen the kiss, she moans into my mouth and I start to slide into her warmth. Clarke groans at the fullness, and my eyes about roll into the back of my head from the tightness of her sheath.

The minute I'm balls deep inside her, reality hits

me. I'm not going to last long. A shudder rips up my spine when Clarke flexes the muscles cradling my cock. Thank fuck I've already made her come twice because, right now, I feel like a schoolboy getting ready to bust a nut for the first time.

Lifting my lips from hers, I mutter, "Hang on, baby."

"Huh?" she asks, but gets no more time to question me, before I pull out and plunge back into her.

God fucking yes... this is what life must be about.

She feels so fucking good, and I can't even attempt to fuck her with slow seduction. Instead, I pull out once more, almost to the tip, then dive right back inside her tight wet heat. My head drops, my forehead resting against hers, and I start pumping between her legs.

In response, Clarke spreads herself wider, pressing her knees to my ribs and sinking her nails into my ass. The tiny bites of pain from those sharp little claws cause me to fuck her just a bit harder, but her grunts of approval assure me that's what she was aiming for all along.

As boldly exciting as it was to finger fuck her to orgasm in her living room, and as sweet as it was to make her come apart with my tongue, there is nothing that could get me to hold back from the deep fucking I'm giving her now.

I absolutely can't control myself, and my body just

takes over.

"You. Okay?" I manage to grind out, my jaw clenched tight as I pound harder between her creamy thighs.

"God, yes," she pants, her palms now flat against my ass as she urges me to go even deeper.

I lift my head, gazing down at Clarke in amazement. Who would have thought she'd like it a bit rough in the end?

It suits me just fine because I like it any way she'll give it. Later tonight, after I get my wits back, I'm going to fuck her slowly for hours.

"Aaron?" Her plaintive tone has me looking down in concern. "I'm… I'm… I think I'm going to come—"

And with that, she bucks hard and bows her back once more, which I've come to realize is her signature tell that she's coming hard. She's strong enough to lift my hips up right along with hers. The unexpected move throws me off, but only for a second. I slam back into her, pushing her deeper into the mattress. As I register the rippling contractions of her muscles all around me and realize with no small amount of pride that she had three supreme orgasms tonight, my body decides it's time to fall over the edge with her. My balls pulse, then contract as I slam deep into her one last time.

Pressing my face into her neck, I mutter, "Fuck. Fuck. Fuck, that feels good."

◆

VERY LONG MOMENTS later, when our breaths have returned to normal and I have Clarke tucked into my side, she makes a small sound in the back of her throat as if she has something to say.

The fingers on one hand, which were stroking her shoulder, still to wait her out. When she doesn't say anything, I ask, "Are you okay?"

Clarke giggles, and it doesn't sound like her at all. I take it to be nerves rather than an airhead-type thing.

In an attempt to put her at ease, because let's face it—what we just shared was fucking intense—I say, "I think I've finally gotten my heart rate to a point I'm confident I'm not going to keel over and die."

Silence continues to reign, but then she finally murmurs, "It was really, really good."

Chuckling, I pull her in tighter.

She coughs slightly, turns more to her side, then lifts her head to look directly at me. "I'm going to ask a really stupid question, and I want you to just chalk it up to the fact I'm not quite as experienced as I thought I was since... well... you know the incident."

"No such thing as a stupid question," I assure her.

"And I don't want you to think I'm making a big deal about anything, because I'm not... I swear."

Patiently, I wait for her to get the guts to tell me what's on her mind.

She lets out a shaky breath. Her cheeks bloom with color, indicating she's incredibly embarrassed. "Do you... um... do you make all women... um... oh, God."

She ends up burying her face in my chest, too cute by anyone's standard in her embarrassment. So I help her out. "Do all the women I'm with end up coming three times?"

"Not just three times," she mutters against my breastbone. "Three stupendous, extremely forceful times."

Got to admit, my ego blooms and expands, swelling under her praise. But still, I have to admit to choosing my words very carefully. "Let's just say I don't normally spend that amount of time on a woman."

"Oh," she murmurs, lifting her head to finally scan my face. I won't tell her the exact truth, which is I've never spent that much dedicated time on a woman before. Sure, I want to make sure any woman I'm with gets off and has a great time, but tonight... I was driven to make Clarke shoot over the moon.

"But..." I continue as I press a quick kiss to the corner of her mouth. "I enjoyed that so much, and I'm looking forward to seeing if I can outdo myself next time."

Clarke's grin seems to harness the entire power of the sun within it. Without hesitation, she smacks a kiss on my mouth.

"Hey, I got an idea," I say, struck with sudden inspiration that's probably foolish, but there's no taking it back now. "Why don't you come with me to Brooke and Bishop's wedding Monday?"

This wedding isn't news to her. We've discussed it, and she knows I'm going to St. John where Brooke and Bishop have rented out an entire resort. I've already informed her I'll be gone for five days. At one point, she'd even told me she was jealous. It's how I found out she doesn't get to travel much. In fact, she hasn't taken a vacation in a couple of years.

"Oh, that sounds so awesome, but there's no way—" she starts, without even giving it serious thought.

It's why I cut her off with a kiss, rolling her to her back. When her legs spread, I settle in between them, peering down with a stern look. "You could use some time away, Clarke. You're the hardest working person I know. You only take off one day a week. And let's be honest, you don't even really take that day off since you admitted you work from home on your books on those days."

"It's hard running a business alone. There's no way I can be away from the store for that long. Nina can only give me part-time hours—"

"Veronica would gladly step in, and you know it," I admonish.

Clarke doesn't snap a comeback because she knows I'm right. Veronica would gladly mind the store, and she's capable of watching it well.

"Clarke," I murmur, tilting my head and giving her a small smile. "You said you wish you could be more spontaneous, and what could be more spontaneous than agreeing to jet off to a tropical island with me for a week? We'll relax on the sand, make love for hours on end, eat all the best foods, and, hey... drink all the fruity cocktails, too."

"It sounds divine," she breathes out dreamily.

"You deserve a vacation," I continue. "I've already got a room there all to myself, so it won't cost you anything. I'll cover your plane ticket—"

"I'll buy my own plane ticket," she pipes up primly. It's then I realize...she just committed.

"*Yes*," I exclaim in triumph.

"Wait... I didn't say I was going."

"Yes, you did. You said you'd buy your own plane ticket. I'm all for equality, but I'm buying meals and a few skimpy bikinis for you to wear."

"But I didn't say—"

I shut her up with my mouth on hers. When I come up for air, she's in a daze, because our kissing is just that good.

"Say you'll come with me," I murmur. "I don't want to be away from you next week."

I can see her melt, her smile turning gooey and her legs lifting to wrap around my waist. She reaches up, tugs at a lock of my hair, and whispers, "It's a good thing you're charming and cute. Otherwise, I wouldn't be going."

"It's the promise of orgasms that changed your mind, admit it," I counter.

She doesn't respond, but merely slips her hands behind my neck and draws my lips down to hers.

CHAPTER 16

Wylde

I HAVE TO give it to Brooke and Bishop. They picked an amazing spot for a destination wedding. The resort is remote and exclusive, spread out over a jutting peninsula off the main island of St. John and on the edge of the Virgin Islands National Park.

Bishop described the place as low key and unplugged, noting there is Wi-Fi, but it's spotty and only accessible from higher ground. There are no TVs in any of the rooms, but plenty of hammocks to lounge in scattered around the one-hundred-acre property.

As a member of a championship hockey team, Bishop can afford the luxury. As such, he paid an exorbitant fee to reserve the resort for the entire week for their wedding party and friends who would be making the trip. Given the size of our team, coaching staff, and support personnel who were invited—including the entire administrative and marketing departments since

Brooke worked there herself—my understanding is this wedding managed to fill the entire place almost to capacity.

Despite such extravagances, I'd been amused when Bishop told me that beyond picking this place for their destination wedding, they'd made very few other choices. They'd left it to the expert staff to plan the food and wedding festivities, including choices for the cake, flowers, and decorations for the seaside ceremony that would take place on a cliff overlooking the brilliant aqua waters of Caneel Bay.

The main building where we check-in is bright and airy, with all the doors and windows open to let in the island breeze. There are potted palms and tropical arrangements placed all around to give the interior that lush jungle feel.

Beside me, Clarke couldn't look any more out of place. I think she's somewhat in shock over the luxury being bestowed upon her. She was agog we flew first class—her first time ever—and the opulence of this resort has her a bit quiet right now.

We wait in a short line at the reception desk to check-in, right behind Pepper and Legend. They're both on FaceTime with Legend's parents, who flew into Phoenix for the week to watch their granddaughter, Charlie. I don't know Charlie's exact date of birth, but she has to be about six months old by now. Over

Legend's shoulder, I can see her cute baby cheeks on the screen of the phone as he and Pepper coo and make baby talk.

The single guy with no interest in thinking about kids at this point in his life would think they're beyond foolish acting, but the man who knows exactly how precious that kid is would never begrudge them one ounce of baby talk. Legend had, unbeknownst to him, gotten a woman, who turned out to be a little nutso in the head, pregnant. She dropped the baby—that would be Charlie—off on his doorstep with a note saying she couldn't take care of an infant anymore, which is how Legend became a father.

Later, Pepper became her mother, the adoption being formally finalized just last month after Charlie's birth mother signed away her parental rights. Of course, the woman's in prison for trying to kill Pepper, but that's a whole other story.

I lean down to put my mouth close to Clarke's ear. "What do you want to do after we check-in?" I ask, leaning in a tiny bit closer so I can brush my lips against her neck. She has her hair up in a ponytail, and I can't resist the bare skin there. Clarke jumps slightly, turning her head to smirk. I give her a wink. "We could test out the resiliency of the mattress in our room?"

She snorts, crosses her arms over her chest as if irritated, and takes a firm step away from me.

She can play offended all she wants, but I know she likes that idea very much. Granted, while she worked her ass off over the past three days to get the store in good-enough shape to entrust the keys to her best friend, Clarke's downtime was spent flat on her back and underneath me. I honestly have never had so much sex in such a short period of time, but I swear it's like the fucking dam has broken. I cannot contain the raging lust for this woman that she's set free.

"Or," I suggest, shuffling closer and putting my arm around her waist. "We could hit the beach. Just relax for the afternoon. Maybe drink a few fruity cocktails."

Clarke giggles, nestling into my side. She angles her face slightly, speaking from the side of her mouth in a low murmur, "I like the testing-the-mattress idea best."

"That's my girl," I praise, pressing my lips to the top of her flame-colored head.

I hear the chorus of female laughter long before the group comes into view. Clarke and I turn that way, seeing Willow, Regan, and Brooke strolling through the lobby. They've clearly settled in nicely, all three wearing summery dresses that show a lot of bare shoulders and legs. Each carries a frothy-looking drink with an umbrella in it.

Regan's eyes land on Clarke and me, and she smiles broadly in welcome. "Oh my God," Regan exclaims as they redirect over our way, focused only on Clarke. She looks inquisitive. "How in the world did this guy talk you into coming so last minute?"

Clarke blushes, remembering exactly how I convinced her, but she merely shrugs while playing it off. "Oh, a free vacation to a tropical island. Wasn't much of a choice, right?"

Willow and Brooke move in, each lady pulling Clarke into a warm hug of welcome.

"Listen," Regan says, reaching out and taking Clarke by the wrist. "We have a spa appointment booked in about forty-five minutes. I know we can get you added. Come spend the afternoon getting pampered with us."

I glare at Regan, and she must feel the weight of it. She shoots me a smirk before giving her attention back to Clarke to entice her further. "Manis, pedis, facials, and massages. An afternoon of pure indulgence."

Yup… going to kill Regan, as she's going way overboard. I had sent a text to the guys the day after Clarke agreed to come with me, asking if they'd ask their women to pay some attention to Clarke so she would feel included instead of like an outsider. It's a request I probably didn't have to make as the Vengeance women are all sweet, kind, and overly generous with their time and concern.

Still, Regan's now interfering with my plans to spend an indulgent afternoon of my own with Clarke in our room. And these resort rooms are off the hook, each with their own private balconies and a half-indoor/half-outdoor lap pool and hot tub. Water is going to be our new best friend in our sexcapades.

Clarke tips her face my way, eyebrows raised in question. I doubt she's ever treated herself to a facial or a massage. Not that she's broke—though she's frugal because she needs to be while owning her own business—but mainly because she rarely takes the time to do nice things for herself.

I bend slightly, putting my hand around the nape of her neck. "You should go relax with the girls. We have five days to test out that mattress."

Clarke's face clouds with worry, a bit of embarrassment tinging her cheeks. She murmurs so only I can hear her, "Do you know how much something like this costs?"

Fuck.

Clarke is a proud woman and it took a lot of damn browbeating to get her to accept my offer to come here without an agreement that she would cover some of her expenses. For example, she didn't want to pay for first-class. However, I already had my ticket purchased, and I wasn't about to ride in coach. We compromised, and she let me pay the difference in costs.

I take her by the elbow, glancing over her head at Regan, Willow, and Brooke before leading Clarke a few steps away. I need to nip this shit in the bud so Clarke can just have a good time instead of second-guessing everything.

"My contract with the Vengeance is a four-year deal worth thirty-two million dollars," I say bluntly.

Clarke goes pale, her mouth dropping open.

I pull her a little farther away, dipping my face closer to hers. "Listen… I get you work hard for what you have, and I also get that what you and I have going on is very new. But I want you to have a great time this week, and I'd like to treat you to this trip. I make so much freaking money it would be the equivalent of a regular Joe buying you a dozen roses for the hell of it. It's a drop in the bucket."

She just stares, face blank and unaffected by my words. I worry I've offended her, so I rush to ask, "Was that pretentious? Because I didn't mean it that way. I just want to make you feel special, I want you to have an amazing week, and I want you to do it without one single worry in your pretty head."

Clarke glances over her shoulder at the waiting women, then back. Her hand comes to my chest, and she tips her head back so her eyes meet mine. There's a soft smile on her lips. "I think what you just said was incredibly sexy, not pretentious at all. And that's me, trying to let go of my past and realize you are you, and not like anyone else I've ever known. So, I will accept their invitation and your generous offer, and I will make it up to you this evening where we will not only attempt to test the mattress, but we will also endeavor to break the bed."

I'm sure if Clarke and I end up becoming a permanent thing—that lasts the test of time like some of my other teammates have been fortunate enough to find—I know I'll look back on this moment, and those words she just gave me, and realize this is probably the beginning of when I really began to fall for her.

"Sounds like a plan," I murmur before giving her a deep kiss filled with the promise of better things to come. It's apparently such a good kiss—perhaps not the type to be made in public—that I'm vaguely aware of the ladies nearby giggling.

I let Clarke up from the power of my mouth, loving that dazed expression she often gets when I kiss her, and make a show of turning her toward the women. Giving her a pat on her ass, I push her toward them. "Might as well get going. Start hanging out with them now. Those drinks look great."

Clarke grins over her shoulder, then moves off to join what looks like a hell of a lot of trouble. Brooke loops her arm through Clarke's. They all take off through the lobby, disappearing through a side door.

"Are you ready to check-in, sir?" I hear from the reception desk, realizing it's my turn. Snickers from behind me have me pivoting, and I see some of the young pups there. Two of the rookies—Vance Gather and Trace LaForge—appear incredibly amused.

"Shut up," I growl.

CHAPTER 17

Clarke

I FEEL OUT of place, yet, I don't.

The glass of champagne in my hand will be my start toward making me feel more comfortable, but the part that's freaking me out the most is being in an alien environment. I'm naked under a plush, white robe while my feet are being scrubbed, pumiced, and polished. We're in a large room with subtle lighting and eight pedicure chairs complete with bubbling feet basins and massagers in the backs.

The chairs are laid out four on each side of the room. Willow, Pepper, Regan, and Nora sit opposite me with Brooke to my left and Blue—who flew straight here from her honeymoon in Australia—to my right. She's currently recounting her terror at going snorkeling with Eric, afraid a shark would eat her but committing to the adventure anyway because he'd really wanted to do it. I found out she's pregnant, which is why she's the only one sipping guava juice instead of champagne.

The women themselves cause a conundrum in me. They are all warm and inclusive, making me feel welcome. But they're also a tight-knit group—women who have all clearly bonded over the last year their significant others have played hockey together. I'm grateful to be included, yet I feel like such an outsider at the same time.

"How did you and Erik meet?" I ask Blue.

She shifts slightly in her seat, shooting me a devilish smirk. "Actually... he and I hooked up years ago, then reconnected last year on the team plane. I'm a flight attendant."

"Second-chance romance," I reply, noting one of my favorite tropes to read.

"Hardly," Blue snorts. "He didn't even remember our time together. It was insulting."

I stare, my mouth agape, and wonder how she found it within herself to ever move past that. But before I can be so nosy as to ask, Pepper chimes in. "Insulting is trying to get a rise out of your hot neighbor by planting dozens of plastic pink flamingos in his lawn, but not even getting a flinch."

The girls laugh. I chuckle, envisioning that. I'm going to assume Pepper had the hots for Legend, but maybe he was playing a little hard to get. Aaron had actually told me a little bit about the circumstances

also owns a professional basketball team.

"Oh yes," Regan drawls, making a strenuous roll of her eyes at Willow. "Your man is so annoying. I mean... he leaves during the playoffs to fly halfway across the world to rescue you from terrorists. I don't know how you ever put up with him."

The other women snicker, but I stare at Willow with abject fascination. "He rescued you from terrorists?"

Willow's expression softens, turning dreamy before she admits, "Well, that might be a slight exaggeration, as I'd already been saved by the time he arrived, but he did leave during the playoffs and fly to Turkey to come get me."

"And then immediately carted you off to Vegas for a wedding," Pepper adds, her own voice sounding dreamy from the romanticism of it all.

"Then off to a luxurious honeymoon in the Maldives," Blue quips. "I hate you by the way."

"I really did score big with Dominik, didn't I?" Willow chirps with a dopey smile.

She gets an "amen," a "preach," and a high snap over a shoulder in agreement. I'm amazed and a little bit in awe of Willow. Somehow, I think these little tidbits I'm getting—brief peeks into these women's love affairs—are really just the tip of the iceberg.

"While I believe all of our stories are fascinating,"

Willow drawls, turning her attention squarely back to me. "I think Clarke needs to tell us how she managed to nab the league's most notorious playboy?"

Really? Most notorious playboy?

"There's a reason they call him Wylde," Regan chortles.

"I'm glad my man handed that title over," Blue mutters.

"He's not all that wild," Brook observes, then gives me a very pointed look. "That man is smitten with you. So how did you meet?"

I'm not sure about the smitten part, but we do have a good meet-cute, that's for sure.

I take a sip of my champagne, then settle in to tell them the story of how Aaron walked into my store and suckered me into a bet that would assuredly land him with two wedding dates.

"Oh my God," Nora exclaims. She's been very quiet up until now. I know her man, Tacker, is Aaron's best friend so I kind of thought she might have already known this story. But then again, I have no clue what Aaron has told his teammates. "That is like the best story ever. I thought Wylde might have layers to him... I just never knew they'd be so multi-dimensional."

"He can quote literary classics?" Blue asks, her eyebrows knitted in confusion. "I thought it was like physically impossible for athletes to be so well-read."

"Stereotype much?" Regan chides.

Blushing, Blue shrugs. "Hey... I'm blonde and I'm not well-read like that. I'm a walking stereotype. I just mean... we all know how much effort our men have to put into this career. It's more than a full-time job. When would he have time to read?"

"Well, regardless," Brooke intones, bringing the subject back around. "I think it's adorable how you two met, and I'm glad things are working out. I think I speak for all the women in this group when I say it's a pleasure watching someone like Wylde fall for the first—and hopefully last—time."

Her sentiment has me feeling awfully unsure of myself. While it's been a bit surreal how much my feelings for Aaron have changed in just a few weeks' time, I still can't seem to shake that impending feeling of doom that this could all come crashing down in a heartbeat.

Their pointed reminders of what a playboy he was are certainly not helping.

"Did we say something wrong?" Brooke asks, her hand coming to settle gently on my forearm.

Whatever is on my face, I try to smooth it out because I don't want to cause the bride concern. I don't want to cause *any* concern, as I'm the guest here.

"No," I rush to reassure her with an overly bright— completely fake—smile. "I'm fine, really."

"Because you don't have to worry about that play-boy stuff," she continues. "Aaron is really into you, trust me on that."

"I know he is," I reply, but the dullness in my tone has her frowning. She shoots a pointed look across the room at the women sitting opposite, then brings her worried expression back. She knows there's more to the story. I feel like there's a proverbial bright light shining in my face, and they're on the verge of wrangling a confession out of me.

"So there's this thing that happened to me." I actually blink in surprise at the ease with which those words come out of my mouth, especially since I had no intention of sharing my secret with these women. And yet... I keep talking. "A few years back, I was on this reality TV show called *Celebrity Proposal.*"

I lay it out. All of my pain, shame, and humiliation over what happened. I tell them about the meme and how it haunts me still. How stupid I felt giving up my virginity to a man I had so thoroughly misjudged and how that shadow hangs over me to this day, still influencing my decisions.

Knowing what I now know about Aaron, I can't believe those past experiences almost kept me from exploring something with him.

Oh, the things I would have missed out on.

"I used to watch that show," Nora says quietly, and

all eyes turn to her. "I remember when that happened."

I flush with embarrassment. It's one thing to recount the story, another to know one of these women watched it play out on live TV.

"You have nothing to be ashamed of," she continues, her voice firm. "You did nothing wrong. You merely followed your heart. Sadly, it misled you."

"Did it ever," I affirm.

"The point being," Nora says, and I'm helpless to look away. She's a therapist, so she must know something about which she speaks. "It's an experience that has helped shape you into the person you are today. I'm going to guess that person is someone who is guarded and afraid to take risks. Nothing wrong with that, but just because that's the person you are today doesn't mean it's the person you have to be tomorrow. You've already gone out on a limb by exploring things with Aaron. That means you're willing to spread those wings a bit, which I think is wonderful. Personally, I think you have the right man to do it with."

I give her a wry smile. "Even though you all call him Wylde? Even though he's the team playboy?"

"Especially so," Nora retorts with a giggle. "Nothing like watching a man like that fall."

The other women agree. More "amens" and "mmm-hmms," and another snap over the shoulder.

"I'm glad you shared that with us," Brooke says,

patting me on the thigh. "You're one of the girls now. An official member of the Vengeance family."

I'm really not since I've only been dating Aaron for a few weeks now, but the sentiment is silly sweet.

"Here, here," the other women proclaim, holding up their champagne glasses.

"By the way," Pepper says, and I can tell by the tone of her voice the subject is changing, for which I'm glad. "Did you guys know Rafe is coming, and he's bringing his new fiancée?"

"Fiancée?" Willow exclaims. "He's only been gone for a couple of months. How does he have a fiancée already?"

"Says the woman who jetted off to Vegas to marry a man she's only known for a few months," Regan mutters out of the side of her mouth to Nora, who snorts loudly.

Willow shoots Regan a glare, then looks back to Pepper for the answer to her question. Pepper shrugs. "No clue."

"We'll find out tomorrow, I suppose," Brooke says, then drains the last of her champagne. An attendant materializes out of nowhere, refilling her glass before moving among the women to top us off.

The bubbly is already making me a little lightheaded, and I wonder what Aaron will do if I show back up at our room completely drunk later. Either things will get really crazy or I'll be a complete dud.

Regardless, I do know one thing with surety. It speaks to the fact I am willing to judge Aaron on his own merits instead of based on my past experiences.

Regardless of the shape I show up in to our room later, Aaron will make sure I'm taken care of and protected. He would, in no way, take advantage of me.

The fact I can admit that tells me quite a bit about myself.

CHAPTER 18

Wylde

I'M NOT A romantic type of guy. Scenery is lost on me. Details like flowers and wedding dress lace don't mean a thing. But as I look around at the wedding reception, which is in full progress, I can't really think of a more appropriate place to tie two lives together.

Today, Brooke and Bishop got married on a bluff overlooking Caneel Bay. They said their vows right at sunset, so the water was sparkling with orange and gold. There were no chairs to sit upon and no formal aisle by which Brooke made her way to Bishop. Friends and family merely stood around in a large semi-circle facing the Caribbean waters. Brooke pulled up in a resort golf cart, and her father escorted her through the crowd that parted for her procession. She wore a strapless white dress that was lacking any adornment, but which flowed down to her ankles. It swished and rippled with her strides, and her bare feet peeked out as she walked across the lush green grass toward her intended. Bishop stood with his back to the sea, a local pastor from the island of St. Thomas beside him.

And right there, with no fancy music, flowers, or even chairs, they exchanged handwritten vows while guided by the pastor. It was the purest thing I'd ever seen, and I thought… if I ever decide to get married, I'm doing exactly this same thing.

The reception is way fucking cool, held in an old abandoned sugar mill dating back to the 18th century on the resort property. It's nothing more than cobbled brick walls—half having fallen—a refinished wooden floor, and no roof to hide the stars above us. Round tables dot the interior, spilling outside to a large tent set on the lush lawn to accommodate the guests. A full sit-down meal of beef tenderloin and lobster is served, the champagne is never-ending, and there's a DJ who's going to be cranking some jams before long. It promises to be a night of partying and celebration. Thank fuck, we're not leaving until the day after tomorrow because I'm sensing many, many hangovers.

We're somewhere in between the newly married couple's first dance and the cutting of the cake, a mellow time for people to mingle and digest the glorious meal we just had. Clarke sits to my left, looking lovely in a peach-colored dress that hugs her body, has only one sleeve, and is cut fairly low. Not that I mind her glasses in the slightest, but she went with her contacts tonight and is wearing her hair down. But rather than her normal wavy curls, she did something to straighten it so it's sleek and hanging even farther down her back than normal. I expect when we make it back to our room at some point, I'll have it wrapped around my wrist, perhaps while taking her from behind.

I immediately banish that thought, not wanting to sport wood in front of my friends, and take the moment to talk to Rafe. He and his new fiancée, Calliope, flew in yesterday and I've not had a chance to catch up with him yet. Merely some brief introductions right before the wedding, so I was happy to see us seated at the same dinner table, along with Tacker and Nora.

Rafe is someone I got close to toward the end of the season, but for reasons I wouldn't wish upon anyone. Just as the playoffs were gearing up, Rafe's dad got diagnosed with an aggressive form of pancreatic cancer and was given only weeks to live. Through some wrangling of deals between Dominik Carlson and Gray Brannon, the general manager of the Carolina Cold Fury, Rafe got traded to that team to be near his dad as he faced his end-of-life journey.

And now, Rafe is here with a fiancée.

"So, what's the deal?" I ask, shifting to peek past Clarke. I drape my arm casually across the back of her chair, then give a sly wink to Calliope, who sits on his

Relaxed on the beach, came back to the room, and had sex. Went out to dinner, came back, and fucked all night. Went snorkeling, came back, and screwed like bunnies.

I want her now. Always will. I doubt that will ever wane, but as I said, she looks exhausted.

"You look like you could do with a good night's sleep," I mention casually as I come to stand before her.

She tips her head back with a smile. "Actually... I wouldn't mind a dip in our pool to cool off a bit."

"We can do that," I say, holding my hand out to haul her up from the bed. She places her palm against mine. Once she rises, she moves right into my body.

I'm surprised when she wraps her hands around my waist to give me nothing more than an affectionate squeeze, briefly pressing her cheek to my chest. "Thanks for bringing me here this week. Tonight was the most fun I've had in a long time."

I give her a squeeze back, my tone laced with faux offense. "I thought I was the most fun you've had in a long time."

She giggles, bending back to see me. "Individually, yes... you're the most fun. As an event, a date, or whatever you want to call it, but the wedding and reception was a lot of fun tonight."

"Agreed," I say. "Bathing suits or naked in the pool?"

True to Clarke-fashion, she blushes. While she's been naked plenty in front of me, she's still not fully comfortable with it yet. Any time she has gotten naked, it's been at my hands or my direction and in direct preface to us having sex.

A part of our foreplay, so to speak.

"Bathing suits seem kind of silly," she remarks with an impish grin.

"I'll close my eyes while you disrobe if it helps," I offer gallantly, but really... I'm going to watch and she knows it.

"Whatever," she responds cheekily. Then I almost swallow my tongue when she steps back, reaches down to her hips, and tugs her dress straight up her body.

Oh, man... her lingerie is on point and I take every bit of it in as the material moves past her shoulders. Butter-yellow lace panties sit high on her hips, low on her belly, and are completely translucent, proving, once again, she's a real redhead. A matching strapless bra covers her breasts, which have fast become one of my favorite places on her body. When her dress is free and tossed to the bed, she reaches behind her to undo the clasp to her bra.

Most shocking, she does so while maintaining eye contact, a feat I admire as I know she's still having some shy reservations around me.

I have to brace my feet apart to hold my ground,

otherwise, I might pounce on her. My entire body goes tight as she shimmies out of those little panties to stand before me gloriously naked.

Clarke nods as she asks, "Going to join me in the pool?"

I scramble into action, kicking off my shoes. She turns from me, moving over to the edge of the pool that snakes into our room from the outside patio underneath a glass wall that opens fully to the outdoors. Undoing the latch, she slides the door, which comes in four panels and essentially removes the entire wall that separates us from the balcony. I'm just working at my belt when she starts stepping down into the small lap pool. As she had not turned on the lights, that damnable dark water covers up her body as she sinks farther down.

I refuse to be embarrassed by my own hard-on that sprang forth while watching her undress, figuring the cool water will tame it into submission. When I'm naked, I follow her into the pool.

The pool is only about five feet in depth, something I can easily walk the length of. Clarke is barely over five feet, so she has to move on her tippy toes or swim it, but I find her at the far end that extends onto the balcony.

The way the rooms are situated—built into an incline of a mountain with privacy walls on either side—we could be laying out on the balcony deck buck naked and no one would see us.

The rooms to our left and right are completely shielded, but sound carries so I keep my voice low as I move to her end of the pool. "Did you want anything else to drink tonight?"

She shakes her head, spreading her arms out along the ledge of the pool behind her. "Just some water before we go to sleep. I have a feeling we're both going to be a little hungover."

That's the truth. I've got a good buzz going on now, and I know she does as well. I credit part of that with giving her the courage to strip down in front of me for the first time without my assistance and for us to do nothing more than take a cooling dip in the pool.

I wade through the water, which barely hits my shoulders, and come to stop in front of her. Bending my knees, I dip my entire body under the water and when I come up, I wipe the water from my eyes, seeing Clarke's smile. The lighting out here is strictly moonlight and two dim sconces, one on each privacy wall to our left and right, but I can tell she's feeling mellow and relaxed.

I actually am, too, despite the heat that had been coursing through me over her naked body moments ago. Slipping my hands under her arms, I grip onto the wall and keep a foot in between us. I can feel her legs treading slightly between my own, her feet sometimes brushing against my shins.

"Can I ask you a question?" she says, her arms now

moving and her hands coming to rest on my shoulders.

"Of course," I say.

"After dinner tonight, you and Rafe were talking about your dads. Your dad died?"

"Yeah," I say, my voice dipping low as I force the acknowledgment up and out. "A few years ago."

Her hands glide back and forth along the skin of my shoulders, almost in a soothing way. "You don't have to share with me if you don't want to."

My hands move under the cool water to her waist. I consider just kissing her to move on from this subject, letting my actions be the answer to her curiosities about my dad. It's going to lead to more about my mom, two subjects I don't like to talk about. The only reason Rafe is privy, and even he doesn't know the full story, is I knew he was in pain and needed the guidance.

Still, as I look at Clarke's face and see nothing but concern mixed with curiosity—not the salacious type but rather born of a need to know me a bit deeper—I realize I've got nothing to be ashamed of by letting her know about my past. The connection I've formed with Clarke has deepened day by day, and I have no reason to hide anything from her.

"My dad was a drunk while I was growing up," I say. By the way her eyes grow round, I can tell I've caught her completely off guard. "He wasn't mean or violent when he drank. Just extremely apathetic. He didn't care about his family, me in particular. He drank a lot… every day after teaching at school… and he'd just sit in his office and ignore my mom and me. Now, granted… my mom was a drinker too, but she did not ignore me. Quite the opposite… she tried to overcompensate for my father's lack of interest. She was oppressive, really."

"I'm… so sorry," Clarke says, aghast at my revelation.

I lean in, kissing her softly. "You don't need to apologize. And his drinking really wasn't the worst of it. Turns out, he ended up having an affair and falling in love with another woman. He left my mother and me when I was fourteen. He got sober—a requirement from his new wife—and started an entire new life without us."

"You said you have a sister," she remembers.

"She's twelve years old now."

"Wow," she murmurs. "And you're not close?"

I gaze into the starry night, seeing the bay sparkling in the moonlight below. "You know how I can quote the classics? Well, that was my pathetic attempt to have a relationship with my dad after he left us. I started reading all his favorites, which he'd left behind. I mean, the man loved those books like nothing in the world, yet he left them all behind when he started a new life. I'd read them, memorize passages, then I'd call him to try to discuss them with him. And he was sober, you know? So I thought he'd enjoy a mutual interest with me, but he didn't care. All he cared about was his new wife and baby daughter. I spent years trying to have a relationship with him over those fucking books, and it was like trying to pull teeth."

"And you eventually gave up," she surmises, sadness evident not only in her tone, but also in the way her arms start to gather in tighter around me.

"He never let me be a part of his new family, so I never got the chance to be close to my sister. When I was eighteen… I just packed the books away in a box and that was when I let my dad go. We rarely spoke after that."

"I know he's dead, but he sounds like an ass," she says hotly.

"Yeah," I agree, her offense on my behalf making me chuckle. "He was an ass. Not a good father at all. At least not to me."

"But you were with him when he died?" she guesses, based on the statements I'd made to Rafe.

"He was pretty sick when he reached out," I say, remembering how shocking it was to not only hear from him, but also to hear he was dying. "I think he was trying to make amends before he died, so I went to see him. He was under hospice care, and I stayed there until he died. He apologized, and I accepted it."

"That was very noble of you," she murmurs.

I shrug, because it really wasn't that transformative for me. His apology was too late, but I'd graciously accepted it to give the man peace. It was the advice I'd imparted to Rafe... help his dad with the transition as best he could.

While I'm glad I was able to freely tell Clarke this, showing her a little bit more of the man I've asked her to trust, I'm also tired of the conversation. There's never anything good in remembering my father didn't care about me in any way until the very end when he only wanted to ease his conscience.

Nor is there any use in telling her that my mom wasn't much better, sinking more into alcoholism after my dad left and that we have virtually no real relationship now.

What I do know is I have a beautiful, sweet, and caring woman in my arms who is very naked. I also haven't seen her yawn once since we got back to the room, so I'm not feeling all that gallant right now thinking she's better served by getting a good night's sleep.

My theory is we can sleep in tomorrow.

Dipping down slightly, I move my hands from her waist to her armpits, lifting her out of the water. She gives a startled yelp, pushing down hard on my shoulders for leverage. Within moments, I have her ass sitting on the edge of the pool. Water sluices down her naked body. I put a large hand to the center of her chest, forcing her to lie down on the wooden decking of our balcony.

She resists for a moment, but ultimately gives in.

And as she slowly leans back, using her elbows to help lower herself down, I note her legs willingly parting so I can step in between them.

The most perfect way to end the evening.

CHAPTER 19

Clarke

I'M SLEEPING SO deeply the first thing I register is irritation that I'm being brought out of it. A sound plays in my head... repetitively at the same pace.

There it is again.

Tap, tap, tap.

I growl in my throat, burrowing deeper against the warm skin and solid muscle of Aaron's arms surrounding me.

"Make it go away," I mutter grumpily, because there is no way in hell I'm ready to wake up. Someone who shall not be named but who is insanely handsome and very good with his hands, tongue, and other body parts kept me up until the wee hours of the morning.

I feel a rumble in Aaron's chest, realizing it's him chuckling, and I vaguely recognize the sensation of his lips pressing into the top of my head.

Then he's gone, a startling chill left where his body

was, and I'm fully awake. I sit partially up in the bed—naked, of course—and press an elbow into the mattress. Rubbing at my eyes, I hastily reach over to the nightstand to put my glasses on so I can clearly see Aaron's gorgeous naked backside walking from the bed toward the door. He nabs a bathrobe from the closet as he passes, and I frown as his body is covered.

Oh, God... I've turned into a certifiable sex fiend, and it's all his fault.

I stretch as Aaron answers the door, noting he doesn't open it very far to afford me privacy, but I still pull the sheet up and over me. I give a stretch, feeling all the ways in which my body is sore from our all-night lovemaking.

Aaron murmurs something to the person on the other side and I flop back down onto the pillow, staring up at the ceiling. When Aaron comes back to bed, I wonder what would happen if I made a move on him.

I've never done that before, as he's always the first to initiate.

Would he be receptive?

Would he be too tired?

Would he think I'm loose and amoral?

I snicker at that last thought. I've come to know Aaron pretty well over the last few weeks we've spent time together, and I'm pretty sure he'd welcome an advance from me.

I think I'll do it.

But shit… should I get up and brush my teeth? Plus, I have to pee. While I'm getting more at ease being naked in front of him, would it look weird for me to get up and jet quickly into the bathroom?

The sound of the door closing has my head popping off the pillow and Aaron strides back to the bed. In his hands is a picnic basket with a card on top.

"What's that?" I ask.

He shrugs. "No clue. It was just delivered, and we were told to open it immediately."

I scramble up in the bed, bringing the sheet with me to cover my breasts. Aaron places a knee to the mattress, then climbs in beside me. I try to ignore the way the robe parts, giving me a peek of golden chest above and his magnificent endowment down below.

He smiles. "You look so cute in the morning with your hair all messed up and those glasses on."

I roll my eyes, scooting in closer to him, then nod at the envelope. "Open it up."

The envelope is square, white, and secured through a hole in the corner via a pretty yellow ribbon tied to the handle of the picnic basket. He removes it, opens the flap, and pulls out a thick piece of cardstock with a handwritten note.

Dear Aaron and Clarke,

Please join us at the seaside bluff overlooking Ca-neel Bay at ten sharp for a very special gathering of friends. Until then, enjoy breakfast on us, which is provided in the basket.

See you at ten.

Love,
Tacker and Nora

"Screw that," Aaron mutters, tossing the card over his shoulder and setting the basket on the floor. Whipping my way, he pounces on me. Burying his face into my neck and pushing the sheet off my body, he murmurs in a way that makes my entire body melt, "I love my friends and all, but I'd rather spend all morning in bed with you."

I laugh, broken by a thoroughly horrid giggle as his stubble tickles my neck, and let my fingers dive in. His mouth feels good, and I know how very much he likes to use his mouth on me everywhere.

But a thought strikes me. "You don't think this is something more meaningful than just a gathering of friends, do you?"

Aaron lifts his head with a frown. "Like what?"

"Like," I drawl with a slight shrug. "It seems wedding fever is sort of in the air with you Vengeance people. Maybe they decided to just get married."

"They're not even engaged," he replies, his frown deepening.

I give him a slight punch to the shoulder, accompanied with a smirk. "For someone who preaches about spontaneity all the time, you don't seem to understand it yourself. You don't have to be engaged to get married, you dork. You can just decide to go for it."

Aaron considers this for a thoughtful moment, then shakes his head in vigorous denial. "No way. They've only been together for like... four months."

"So?" I reply blandly. "My parents dated less than two months before they got married."

His gaze goes a little fuzzy as he considers this, but then he refocuses. "No. Just no way. Tacker's got too much wedding baggage to do something like this so suddenly."

My chin pulls inward with confusion. "Wedding baggage?"

Aaron rolls off me, balancing on his arm and his hand lazily comes to my stomach to rest there. His expression is somber. "Tacker has come through a lot of painful stuff over the last few years. He was piloting a small aircraft with his fiancée aboard. They crashed, and she died. This was before he came to the Vengeance. And through most of last season, he just spiraled. Was really drowning in grief he couldn't process."

I had briefly heard this story before—from Aaron in

passing, but Nora had also mentioned it the first day we were here. I hadn't asked any questions, though, as that was something so personal I didn't want to pry.

"He was so lost," Aaron muses. He's obviously sharing the story with me, but I can tell he's a million miles away and lost in his memories. He and Tacker are best friends, so I'm sure Aaron witnessed the worst. "I wasn't sure he'd ever recover, and while I know he loves Nora with all his heart and soul, wouldn't he still be terrified at the thought of marriage? Wouldn't he be scared it could happen again?"

"So, you think it's too soon?" I ask.

He throws it back on me, clearly not sure about anything. "Isn't it?"

"Not if they love each other and they're sure about it." Of this, I'm certain. I believe when something is real, a person knows it deep down inside. And I know this because if I'm honest with myself, the terrible little secret I carry around with me is I wasn't sure about giving my virginity up to Tripp on that stupid reality show. I'd had doubts, but I felt so pressured to play the game.

I'll never make that mistake again.

Suddenly, Aaron explodes upward, gazing at me with wonder. "They're going to get married."

I grin. He seems certain of it now, and his goofy expression of joy is beautiful. It speaks to how much he loves his friend, Tacker.

"Can't believe the rat bastard didn't share this with me, though," Aaron muses, still grinning with affection in his tone.

"Maybe it was so spontaneous they just decided last night?" I suggest.

Aaron doesn't respond, but glances past me to the bedside clock. "It's almost eight."

I look between the clock and Aaron, whose expression changes drastically in just that second or two it takes my head to swivel one way and then back again. His eyes are dark, glittering, and predatory.

A shiver of excitement runs through me. I decide to be bold, letting my fingers play at the collar of his robe. "I'm going to go pee. Then I think you and I have plenty of time to bang out an orgasm or two before we head to the bluff."

Aaron's gaze lights up with an almost feverish glitter as he practically pushes me out of bed. "Hurry. We also have whatever's in that basket to eat, too."

Laughing, I'm not even the slightest bit self-conscious as I slip out of bed buck naked and practically prance to the bathroom. I can feel the weight of Aaron's gaze on me, and it feels good.

◆

As we walk the paths of the resort toward the same

bluff Brooke and Bishop got married on just yesterday, we don't pass anyone else. This seems to indicate if Tacker and Nora are indeed getting married, the invitations that went out were limited.

We traverse up a gentle rise, the bluff at the top. I take in the handful of people. By doing a quick perusal and pairing it with the recent hockey knowledge Aaron's been teaching me, it appears that only the Vengeance first line was invited, along with the team's owner.

Aaron and I weren't sure what to wear, but given the impromptu nature of whatever this is, plus the fact Tacker and Nora are extremely laid-back people, we dressed casually. I chose a floral-print maxi dress in pink, peach, and yellow while Aaron's in navy shorts and a red and white Hawaiian-print shirt. We totally clash with each other, but we don't care.

Dressed equally as casually are Dominik and Willow, Erik and Blue, Legend and Pepper, and Dax and Regan. I'm completely astonished to see Brooke and Bishop, since they are technically on their honeymoon and figured they would want to stay in bed.

"Good morning, everyone," Tacker's booming voice says just as we near the gathered group. Everyone turns his way. He and Nora are walking hand in hand up the knoll, and they are followed by the same minister who performed yesterday's ceremony.

"Yup," Aaron murmurs from the side of his mouth.

"They're getting married."

Of that, there's no doubt. The minister totally gives it away.

There are hugs given out as soon as they reach us, both Tacker and Nora taking a few moments with each guest to thank us for coming on such short notice.

What isn't said but is clear is this group is close. They share bonds that traverse the team dynamics, venturing into almost unexplainable depths.

Nora reaches out, and I take her hands. I get a squeeze and a brilliant smile. "I'm so glad you're here to share this with us."

"I'm so honored," I reply, humbled to so easily be accepted into this group. Granted, it's my association with Aaron that got the invite, but after our pedi date that first day, I know these women will continue to be good friends. I would say even if Aaron and I don't work out, they'll still be a part of my life.

Of course, the thought of Aaron and I not working out causes a sharp, stabbing pain in the center of my chest, which tells me I'm in deep with him already. Amazing how quickly life can change.

Eventually, the minister manages to break up the group love and calls for us to gather around him. Rather than the wedding couple facing us, Tacker and Nora choose to stand with us... their friends gathered at their backs and sides, facing the pastor. The morning sun is bright, periodically faded by bright fluffy clouds overhead. A salty sea breeze tickles my face.

It couldn't be a more beautiful day or setting for a wedding. Even though it's the same exact spot we were in yesterday for a wedding, this feels so different.

It's intimate and spiritual. The love passing between Nora and Tacker as they gaze at each other is almost magical. I realize I'm witnessing something so special I may never see it again.

The minister merely welcomes this private gathering, assuring us the paper legalities have all been handled. "So my part is rather limited this morning. My understanding is the couple merely wishes to exchange the vows they've written, so… Nora, would you like to begin?"

Nora nods, but she doesn't take her eyes off Tacker. She's wearing a simple off-the-shoulder dress in mint green with a subtle cream floral pattern around the hem. It flutters around her tanned legs, her loose hair swirling about her shoulders. The breeze blows a few tendrils into her face. She pushes them behind her ears as she starts her vows.

"Tacker… there was a time in my life where I didn't believe in love, miracles, God, or humanity. While I managed to stumble out of that dark place long ago, there was still always a bit of shadow hanging over me. Perhaps it was just that my true purpose was unknown, but all I know is from the minute you came into my life, nothing has ever been clearer. You're what I've been waiting for. You're the reward I get for all the bad I had to go through. You're my destiny, and you're well worth any pain I've been through to get here. I'm honored to spend the rest of my life with you."

I don't know Nora's back story, but she clearly has one. Within her words, I could feel something terrible must have happened, just as I could feel Tacker has healed up every bit of that. And from what little I know about their situation—the fact that Nora was his counselor—I thought it would have been reversed.

Tacker has a sheen of wetness in his eyes, which he doesn't even bother trying to blink away. He just smiles at Nora as if she's the most glorious thing he's ever beheld, mouthing the words, "I love you," to her in response.

The minister says, "Tacker... your vows."

Tacker releases Nora's hands and gives an apologetic cough as he reaches into his front pant pocket, pulling out a folded piece of paper.

When he unfurls it, I see it's actually several pieces of paper, but they're small... the size of the stationery on the desk in our room.

Holding it up for all to see, he gives Nora a sheepish grin. "I stayed up last night after you went to sleep to play around with some words. I didn't feel like I could

The preacher can't even get the words out before Tacker grabs Nora, dips her low, and plants a long, searing kiss on her.

Everyone erupts into cheers, and I feel wetness on my cheeks. I dash the happy tears with the back of my hand, but not before Aaron catches me. His arm comes around my shoulder and he pulls me into his side, giving me an affectionate squeeze.

CHAPTER 20

Wylde

"**W**HY AM I so nervous?" Clarke whispers from beside me.

I look down at her, hands wringing together nervously while her gaze darts all around her store. This is a change—the standing in place and radiating anxiety—from the frantic dashing around she'd been doing for the past half hour as she tried to make sure everything was perfect for Pepper's book signing.

We've been back from the Virgin Islands for a full week now, and we've settled into a routine. Clarke is back at her store, hard at work for six days a week while on the seventh, she works from home. I loiter as much as she'll tolerate, snagging whatever free time she has in between hanging out with my dudes, amping up my workouts, and generally enjoying the off-season.

Generally enjoying Clarke, really.

I can't figure out the why of it—or even how she

and I are working out—but we are. Each day, we get a little bit closer.

Each day, I realize I can't imagine her not being in my life.

I've stopped the internal musings I'd found myself doing just a week ago, where I'd qualified every thought about Clarke with an "if we make it" mentality.

Now it's not a question of *if*... It's more of a question of *who* and *when*.

Who will be brave enough to first make the assertion to the other that what we have between us is special, real, and meant to last?

I mean... I've done that, internally at least. I've accepted the fact I am no longer the team's playboy, and that I never want to go back to that lifestyle. I simply want what I have with Clarke, and I hope to continue building on it. I can't even imagine there being another woman who excites me as much or makes me as happy as she does.

But I am dealing with a woman who, despite the fact she's now wringing her hands and looking for reassurance, still proves to be a little prickly when it comes to issues of trust. This past week alone, she's clearly been put off when I'm recognized while we are out. It's not that she doesn't trust me to handle a situation, because she's seen just how protective of her I can be when people horn in on our privacy. But she just doesn't like the fame by association that comes with being by my side.

It's something, however, I have great hopes will get better with time.

Reaching out, I take Clarke's hands in mine. "You're going to be fine. This is going to be a great success. I promise."

"How can you promise?" she asks harshly, an edge of hysteria in her voice. She glances over to the table that's been set up for Pepper—who is currently in the bathroom touching up her makeup before we open the doors—and then fearfully regards me. "What was I even thinking by asking someone like Pepper to come to my little bookstore? I mean, sure... I invited my entire customer list, but most don't buy children's books. What if no one shows up? Pepper is going to hate me and—"

There's no other intervention that works quite as well on a distraught woman than a searing kiss meant to distract. This is accomplished with one hand behind her neck, the other on her lower back so she's drawn in tight, and all of my focus and dedication on kissing her properly.

Veronica, who is behind the cash register, snickers. Over this past week, I've come to realize she takes great amusement in watching me fluster her friend. One day, when I was helping stock shelves, she confided that she thinks I'm just the saving grace her bestie needed in her life and she wanted me to know—confidentially, of course—that her loyalties were now solely with me if Clarke ever got squirrely and tried to end this relationship.

I'm not sure how that makes me feel. On one hand, it's nice knowing Clarke's best friend thinks I'm good for her and will work with me to make sure Clarke knows that, too. But on the other, she has to feel there's room for worry by making that proclamation, which means she must have some doubts as to whether Clarke has sticking power with me.

Regardless, I refuse to dwell on future what-ifs. Instead, I focus on kissing my girl senseless.

When I decide she's discombobulated enough to no longer concentrate solely on her anxiety, I let her up for air. Pushing her glasses up her nose, she murmurs, "Well... that was nice."

Still with my hand at her neck, I pull her in close, placing my lips at her ear where I whisper low enough it remains private. "I can certainly take you back to your office for a few minutes before we open those doors and distract you in another way. Guaranteed to mellow you out a bit if you'll let me."

Clarke gasps at the thought, but she immediately pushes me back, muttering harshly. "No way. People would know."

"No one would know," I assure her, but then dart a glance at Veronica. Okay, she'd know, but whatever.

Pepper comes out of the small hallway that leads down to the men and women's bathrooms. She's a striking woman in her own right. Not to my particular taste, but I get why Legend is nuts about her. She has the most amazing light blue eyes, which seem to shimmer against the crop of almost blue-black bangs that cut over her forehead. She wears her glossy hair in a short bob, and she has sort of a schoolgirl-rocker vibe going on with her outfit. In a red wraparound dress with white polka dots and black Doc Martens, she'd used a leather choker with silver spikes around her neck to tie it all together.

She heads over to Clarke and me with a relaxed smile. It starts to turn into a frown as she takes in Clarke, who is practically radiating with nervous anxiety.

"Are you okay?" she asks Clarke, clearly concerned.

"I'm just terrified this is going to be a bust," Clarke answers truthfully.

"No way," Pepper assures her with a careless wave of her hand. "But even if it is, we'll have a great time hanging out. Your store is absolutely charming. I've told several people to come by, so it will be fine."

"I just don't want to let you down," Clarke admits glumly.

I settle my arm around Clarke, intent on drawing her in for a hug. I want to ease her fears, but I can't. We'll have to let this play out.

Before I can even curl my fingers around her waist, someone knocks on the front door of the bookstore, which we've yet to unlock. I glance at the clock, realizing it's already nine.

It's showtime.

Clarke makes a distressed sound in her throat and my gaze jumps to her. She's staring out the glass door and windows at the front of the shop. When I turn that way, a rush of giddiness sweeps through me as I see a long line of people waiting to get in.

Seems the little social media outreach me and some of my teammates conducted worked. I move to the door while Clarke scrambles alongside Pepper to sit at the table. Clarke had ordered a huge shipment of Pepper's most popular children's book, *The Grand Adventures of Penelope and Bert*. Clarke's going to be ringing up books at the table with her mobile device. Veronica's going to cover the register for regular shoppers who might be so generous as to buy something else while here.

I put my hand to the lock, glancing over my shoulder at Clarke and Pepper. "You two ready?"

"Ready," Pepper says with a sound nod of confidence. Clarke looks like she's ready to throw up, but for a completely different reason now. She's no longer worried about no one showing up. Instead, she's now freaking out about taking care of the people amassed outside.

I give her a wink and unlock the door, pulling it wide open. As I stand there, people stream in. I look out the window and down the street. Holy shit... the line's down to the end of the block, and it disappears down the side.

Maybe the boys and I were a little too effusive in our posts yesterday. I had reached out to Tacker, Dax, and Erik and asked if they would share about the book signing on their social media accounts. I didn't bother asking Bishop, who is still back in the Virgin Islands on his honeymoon. I also didn't ask Dominik, because he runs multibillion-dollar businesses and has better things to do. And I certainly didn't need to ask Legend, who had already been posting everywhere about his wife's book signing. But between Tacker, Dax, Erik, and me, we have a social media reach well into the hundreds of thousands, many of whom are here in the Phoenix area. It was my hope we'd interest more than a handful of people to come out, but, turns out, many seem inspired to check out Clarke's store and Pepper's books.

I may have gotten a little personal in my post. On my Instagram, I'd posted a selfie I'd taken of Clarke and me together on the beach at the resort last week. We were leaning in toward each other from our beach chairs, both with big silly grins on our faces. We were sunkissed and carefree looking, but, just before I snapped the picture, I had turned to look at her. My expression could only be described as adoring while Clarke stared right into the camera with a wide smile.

On my post, I'd typed, *Me and my girl in St. John last week. Come by and check out her store, Clarke's Corner.* I'd then put that Pepper would be signing her children's books there, and tagged both Pepper and Legend's accounts. I couldn't tag Clarke as she doesn't have any social media, and I can't say I blame her. I think she realized that what she doesn't know can't hurt her, and it's better to just not look at that stuff.

Regardless, I don't regret my actions since it's evident Pepper's book signing is going to be a huge success while Clarke is going to amass a lot of new customers.

Legend shows up within a few moments of the doors opening, giving Pepper a quick apology for being late. He ran into some traffic issues while dropping Charlie off at her grandparents. He ended up sitting at the table with Pepper and Clarke, sometimes joining Pepper in a picture if a fan requested it. But, for the most part, I'm impressed the people genuinely seem to be here for the author and the bookstore.

I help direct shoppers around the store, having become intimately familiar with where everything is located over the last several weeks of hanging out and helping on occasion. Veronica stays busy at the register. Many customers buy knickknacks or other books after getting their books signed by Pepper.

The signing itself is only supposed to last from nine to twelve, but there is no stopping the influx of people that keep arriving. Pepper generously stays until two. We actually had to cut the line off and lock the doors at one-thirty to stop more people from coming in.

After, we turn out most of the store's interior lights, put the closed sign on the door, and plop down in the reading chairs. Veronica brings a few bottles of champagne she had chilling in the fridge in the back for—in her words, an occasion to celebrate—and pops them effortlessly. She pours plastic cups for herself, Clarke, Legend, Pepper, and me, and we sip while ruminating on the success of the day.

Seeing the satisfaction and joy—albeit in an exhaustingly satisfied type of way—on Clarke's face, I know it's going to be my joy to try to help her in any way I can, whenever I can. It is important she succeeds, so aiding her is now a firm goal of mine.

Clarke leans forward in her chair, still behind the signing table, and looks past Pepper to Legend. "I'm going to assume you might have had something to do with that crowd," she teases him. "Bragging about your wife to all your fans, huh?"

Of course, Clarke would think that. Many people

who came in today knew Legend, as evidenced by the fact they asked for pictures with him, too, after Pepper signed their book. I don't say a word, completely fine with letting Legend take full credit for this.

He merely shrugs, looping his arm around his wife's shoulder. "What can I say? I'm proud of this woman, and I would sing it from the mountaintops if I could."

"Well, thank you," Clarke says with a gracious incline of her head. "That clearly helped bring in the crowd."

"Yeah… thanks, baby," Pepper croons, tipping her head so she can receive a kiss from Legend.

I'm vaguely relieved Clarke thinks this was all Legend's doing, though it does shine a glaring light on an issue that is still pervasively complicated within our relationship. I'm not sure she would have liked me using social media to spotlight her. She's still so very wary about fame and limelight, so she might have been offended if she'd known I'd done it.

Of course, she might have been incredibly grateful, too, but it's not something I would know as I don't intend to tell her what I did. I don't need praise from her, and I certainly don't want her ire. I'm happy to just let well enough ride.

After we finish our champagne, Legend and Pepper leave the store. Veronica and I help clean up, straightening the shelves, and I run the vacuum cleaner. There's no crowd outside when we open the store back up around three.

Veronica takes her leave, so I settle into one of the reading chairs, content to spend the rest of the day here with Clarke. I'm going home with her after Nina comes in for the evening shift, and I have nothing else to do until then.

"I'm going to ask you something, and I hope it doesn't freak you out," Clarke says out of the blue. I've been thumbing through a book of poetry that I'm not connecting with, but I've never really been into it to begin with. That certainly hasn't changed with maturation.

I look up, not concerned in the slightest over her freaking me out. I like her way too much to let anything bother me. "What's up?"

"How would you feel about meeting my parents?" she asks hesitantly.

I blink in surprise, not because this is an unwarranted request or too soon. In fact, it seems about the right time.

I have a moment of shock—maybe more awe than anything—that Clarke clearly thinks this is serious, much in the same way I do, even though we haven't quite yet voiced it to each other yet.

"You know, I've never once in my entire adult life been asked to meet a woman's parents," I reply with a crooked smile.

She rolls her eyes. "I'm not so sure you've bothered asking a woman her last name before."

A bark of laughter erupts from me, and I love she can make light of my reputation. I spring up from my chair and snag her around the waist, pulling her back down into the same chair with me.

"I'd love to meet your parents," I say before inclining my head and pressing my lips to her neck.

CHAPTER 21

Clarke

"STOP FIDGETING," AARON commands and I shoot him a side-eyed glare from the passenger seat of his truck.

"I can't help it," I mutter, but I clasp my hands tightly together in an effort to stop my nervous squirming. "You know how you've never met a woman's parents before?"

Aaron whips his head my way, his gaze on me far too long since he's actually driving, but then he moves his attention back out the windshield. "You mean to tell me you've never brought a man home to meet your parents?"

"Of course I have," I snap, frustrated he isn't getting the significance of my discomfort. "I've brought a few home before."

"Gee," Aaron drawls, his voice dry as the desert floor. "I feel so special."

I snort and grab his hand, which is within reach since his arm is resting casually on the center console. Sliding my fingers between his, I squeeze. "You should feel special, because those other dudes I brought home were easy."

"Not making me feel better," he mutters.

"What I mean is they were all perfectly nice and uncomplicated, so it was easy to bring them over for a dinner with my parents. You're..."

"Not uncomplicated?" he guesses.

I shift to face him. While he doesn't look, keeping his attention firmly on the road, I know I have his full focus by the way he stills. "You're the best kind of complicated. And it makes this visit far more important than any other, which is the reason for my fidgeting."

Aaron finally spares me a glance. "That's the nicest thing you've ever said about me."

"I know, right?" I quip back with a grin. "Who would have thought I'd like complicated?"

Aaron pulls my hand to his mouth, then kisses my palm before drawing it down to rest in his lap for the rest of the ride to my parents' house.

When we arrive, I take a deep breath as Aaron pulls into the driveway behind my father's Cadillac. They still live in the same house I grew up in. Whenever I see the glowing lights within, it always brings me a measure of comfort. My parents have been looking forward to meeting the man I have seemingly taken a big chance on, as I think they've all but given up on me finding someone to have a solid relationship with.

While they fully supported my decision to go on that reality show, I'd known they had trepidations. In their infinite wisdom, they could see the potential for hurt and heartache in a way I just couldn't. However, they also are the type of parents who believe the best way to grow and mature is by making mistakes that sting long enough to make lasting impressions.

When we make it to the porch, the door swings open and my father stands there.

Perry Webber certainly doesn't look like the stereotypical accountant. My father more resembles a beach bum or a surfer dude than an accountant, which, technically, he sort of is. He was raised in southern California, and he could ride a surfboard flawlessly by the time he was five years old. He has longish, wavy blond hair, pale blue eyes, and a thick beard. He's also tall and muscled, almost as broadly built as Aaron.

I can tell Aaron is shocked by his appearance, especially since my dad is wearing faded jeans ripped at both knees, an old Billabong t-shirt, and no shoes.

"You were expecting glasses and a pocket protector, weren't you?" I can't help but tease Aaron in a low voice before making a formal introduction to my father.

Aaron smirks, shaking my father's hand before he

invites us in. My dad leans in to give me a quick peck on the cheek, which tickles, then claps Aaron on the shoulder. "Aaron and I will fix everyone a drink. Your mom is in the kitchen."

"Very subtle, Dad," I mutter, and he winks. I'd expected no less than him pulling Aaron aside for some alone time to judge him. This is something Dad hasn't ever done with someone I've brought over before, but I've told my mom how much I like Aaron. I'm sure she's passed that tidbit along to my father.

I find Mom in the kitchen, making what looks like stir fry. I'm almost a pure clone of Amy Webber and if Aaron ever wants to know what I'll look like in my late forties, he only has to gaze at my mom. We share the same fiery hair, hazel eyes that turn greener with high emotions, and petite frames. Our facial structure is almost identical, and my mom often gets mistaken for my older sister. I sure hope I have her youthful appearance and lack of lines when I'm her age. She always harps on me to wear sunscreen, and I'm mostly diligent about it.

"Hey, baby," my mom coos when she sees me walk in. I round the kitchen island, and we engage in a long hug while the stir fry sizzles in the wok. "I've missed you."

"Missed you back," I assure her as we release. Bending over the wok, I inhale. "Smells good."

My mom smiles, peering through the archway of the kitchen with a raised eyebrow. "Your dad kidnap Aaron already?"

"Yup," I reply, moving back to the end of the counter and perching on a stool. "I'm sure he's grilling him deeply by now."

My mom laughs as she stirs the wok, splashing in soy sauce while her other hand perches on her hip. She's always so relaxed and carefree. I definitely did not inherit that from her, but I do strive to emulate that. "Well, while the boys are otherwise occupied, tell me all about the trip to St. John."

My mom isn't totally clueless. I'd shared photos and texts. We've talked via phone and because I'm super close to my mom, she knows exactly how I feel about Aaron. But we haven't seen each other since I've returned, so I haven't been able to give her all the details.

"It was wonderful," I say, propping my chin in my hand while she cooks. "So relaxing. And Aaron's friends are super nice. The guys he plays on the same line with are all married, and their wives are so outgoing and inclusive. I didn't feel like an outsider at all."

"They sound lovely," she replies.

"They really are." Admittedly, they were so much more than I had anticipated.

I spend some time describing the resort, how we

went snorkeling in crystal waters, and how we dined on some of the best food I've ever had. I did not tell her about how much sex I'd had, the countless orgasms, or how Aaron has taught me more about intimacy and desire than I could have ever learned from any other source because he takes the time to make it good for me. I love my mom and we are indeed close, but not *that* close.

I merely say, "Aaron's great, Mom. I'm really glad I met him."

"And gave him a chance," she points out. "It was a good risk you took."

That's for sure. No one besides my mom and Veronica knows just how badly I was hurt and humiliated by Tripp. I spent what seemed like hours crying in her arms after that whole debacle, and because she's my mom, she hurt right along with me. More than anyone, she's always understood my reluctance to try again.

My dad comes strolling into the kitchen with Aaron on his heels, each carrying two drinks. My dad has a bourbon neat, and he places a glass of white wine on the counter by my mom, taking a moment to press a kiss to her neck as he passes.

Aaron has a beer for himself, and he hands me a glass of white wine. He knows I'm not picky about what I drink, as I like trying all kinds of wines. He comes to stand beside me, leaning forward on the counter.

"Aaron was just telling me how you two met," my father says, his eyes shining with amusement.

My mom snickers, because she knows the story, but she apparently hadn't told my dad about it. Aaron bumps his hip against mine, grinning.

"He totally hustled me," I gripe, giving my dad a pained look.

"I think it's hilarious," my dad replies. "I like a man who does whatever it takes to win his lady."

My dad is the true romantic in our household, that's for sure.

Aaron's phone rings, and he ducks his head in apology as he pulls it from his pocket. "Sorry about that," he murmurs as he puts it on vibrate before placing it on the counter.

"No worries," my dad replies.

"Honey," my mom says, shooting him a look. "Can you grab some plates? We'll just self-serve from the wok, then eat at the kitchen nook. It's cozier than the dining room."

That's how I know my parents like Aaron, and, more importantly, *like* that *I* like him. Otherwise, my mom would have done a formal sit down in our dining room. This way, it's all family style. It's telling that even though my parents don't know that much about him— just a few moments of conversation and my impressions—they can tell he's a good guy.

Aaron's phone starts vibrating on the counter. We both glance down, seeing it's Tacker calling. He hits the button to decline the call, but it immediately starts ringing again.

Aaron glances at me, his face now etched with worry. I nod at the phone. "You better answer that."

No way Tacker's calling three times in a row unless it's important.

"I'm really sorry," Aaron says to my mother, who shakes her head and holds her hand up that it's fine.

Aaron picks up the phone. As he walks from the kitchen into the other room, he says, "What's up?" I'm not sure if I should follow him, but a churning in my gut says this can't be good.

Worriedly, my mom looks at me. I shrug. My dad gets the plates out, but he doesn't say a word as he sets them on the counter. We all sit in silence as we wait for Aaron to return.

When he walks back in, his face is pale, and I immediately push off the stool to go to him. "What happened?"

"It's Baden," he says, staring down before turning to my parents. "He's one of my teammates. Our backup goalie."

My dad nods, because he's a sports nut and follows the Vengeance. To me, Aaron says, "I don't have all the details, but he tried to intervene in a mugging and got attacked."

"Oh my God," I gasp, clutching Aaron's hands. "Is he..."

"He's at the hospital right now and it's pretty bad."

"Jesus," my dad mutters, and my mom turns the stove off.

"I'm really sorry," Aaron says to my parents. "But I really need to get to the hospital. The entire team is congregating there."

"Of course," my mother exclaims, coming around the side of the counter toward us, my dad following behind.

I nab my purse from a chair where I'd set it earlier, but Aaron places a hand on my arm. "You don't have to come. You should stay... have dinner with your folks."

For a moment—a horrible, low moment—I think Aaron doesn't want me to go because I don't belong. This is a team tragedy, which goes beyond me.

But that moment passes, because I can't afford to fall prey to my own self-esteem issues. Not when I can see Aaron is visibly shaken by this news.

Shaking my head, I take his hand. "I'm going with you. And if you trust me with your big behemoth of a truck, I'll drive."

Aaron's expression loses the tightness around his mouth, his eyes going soft and warm. It's gratitude I see reflecting back, and I know he needs me. "I'm glad you're coming, but I'm still driving."

At the door, my mom gives Aaron a big hug and assures him she'll make dinner up to him soon. My dad makes me promise to text them as soon as we hear any news, then gives me another tickling kiss on my cheek. I hold onto him a bit tighter, thankful for their love and support. Aaron doesn't know what it's like to have parents like this, which is also why I feel the pressing need to stay by his side.

My parents stand in the doorway. They watch as Aaron helps me into the truck, and I wave to them through the window as we pull out of the driveway.

When we hit the highway, I ask, "How bad is it?"

Aaron cuts me a short glance, then squeezes my hand. He's been holding it ever since we pulled out, steering assuredly with the other. "Bad. Tacker says from the report he heard, three guys were attacking one woman. When Baden tried to intervene to help her, he was beaten with a crowbar and stabbed."

"Jesus," I murmur, following my curse with a silent but solemn prayer for Baden.

"Dominik and Willow are flying in from Los Angeles on one of Dominik's private planes. He'll get the best doctors from wherever he can to attend to Baden."

I've never liked the privilege that comes with being extremely wealthy, or the elite opportunities that are afforded to them, but, in this moment, I am so very grateful Dominik has those resources. While I don't know Baden all that well, I had some great interaction with him in St. John. He reminds me a lot of Aaron in that laid-back, happy-go-lucky kind of way. A humble, down-to-earth guy.

A man who tries to stop a mugging, who instead ends up stabbed and beaten. A tremor runs up my spine, because that could have easily been Aaron. He would have stepped in if he'd been the one to see that.

The nausea that swells within me at the thought—of something terrible happening to Aaron and me losing him—is nothing more than an affirmation I'm in deep with this guy.

CHAPTER 22

Clarke

I PACE THE small length of my living room, periodically checking my phone. It's been almost twenty-four hours since Aaron and I left my parents' house when we got word about Baden.

I had gone to the hospital with Aaron, and it had been a somber event. Baden had been savagely attacked by three men when he'd tried to stop them from attacking a woman in a downtown parking garage. He had to have emergency surgery as he had multiple stab wounds—seven in all—and he had some bleeding on his brain from where they beat him with a crowbar.

Those wounds were all miraculously stabilized, but were not the worst of the news. The assailant with the crowbar hit him in the back so hard that Baden suffered a spinal cord concussion. He's currently paralyzed from the waist down.

It was horrible news and the weight of grief in the

waiting room—packed with players, coaches, executive staff, and loved ones—was so palpable I felt like I was suffocating at times. Dominik arrived within two hours by private jet, conferenced with the team doctors and Baden's parents, then, with the power of his pull and money, he'd flown in one of the best surgeons in the world who would attempt to stabilize the spinal injury.

It's been hours since I last heard from Aaron, though. I'd stayed at the hospital until just past midnight last night when he'd insisted on taking me home since I had to get up early to open the store. Of course, I refused to let him take me home and had insisted on an Uber. There'd been a back-and-forth argument, then a compromise when Nora offered me a ride as she had to leave due to early appointments the next morning, too.

Baden's surgery lasted throughout the night. He finally came out of it around nine this morning. Aaron kept me apprised via texts throughout the day, but, by noon, everyone was urged to leave and get some rest. Dominik put Baden's parents, who'd flown in from Montreal, up in a hotel and Aaron had told me he was going home for a shower and a nap.

My last communication from him was around three this afternoon and since then... nothing. I have to assume he's still resting, and it's hard to resist the urge to call and wake him up. What I hate the most about this, though, is I am feeling this pressing need to be by his side, if for nothing more than to just be a presence should he need me. Throughout my time at the hospital, I could see how horrific this was for Aaron. Baden isn't just a teammate. He's a brother to them all, so his injury directly struck each of them. I'd never seen Aaron so weighed down with emotion.

Never seen him so quiet and withdrawn, either. I'm not used to it. It's freaking me out, although I simply cannot take it personally. This is a moment in our relationship when we will learn something about each other... how we deal with tragedy.

The knock on my front door startles me so badly I let out a tiny yip of fright. But I immediately know it's Aaron.

Or rather... it *has* to be him.

I practically hurdle over my coffee table as I rush to the door, flipping the lock and swinging it open without even bothering with the peephole.

And damn... he looks awful.

Without thought or hesitation, and without needing to ask the million questions I have burning within, I simply pull him into my house and wrap my arms around him in a hard hug.

I hadn't realized how much I'd needed to feel him until the relief courses through me when he returns my embrace, dipping to rest his cheek on the top of my head for a few moments while we just absorb each other.

Finally, I ask, "Have you gotten any rest?"

"Yeah," he replies, pulling slightly back from me. "About an hour this afternoon. We just had a team meeting, so I thought I'd come by. Hope that's okay?"

"It's always okay," I rush to reassure him. "In fact… would it be weird if I offered you a key?"

His smile is wan, but I can see he likes my offer. "I'll give you a key to my place, too."

"Wow… we are getting serious," I tease.

His smile falters, but only because it's obvious he has bad news. Taking his hand, I lead him around the loveseat to the couch, urging him down. I settle in close beside him, brushing my fingers over his brow as he spreads his legs under the coffee table and leans his head back against the cushion.

"Baden may never walk again," he murmurs, his voice choked with grief.

I move up to my knees until I'm hovering over Aaron. His eyes are closed, his face pinched with pain. I press my lips to his temple. "But he's alive, Aaron. And if there's a chance he might never walk again, then there's a chance he could, right?"

His eyes flutter open and he just stares, his expression devoid of any hope. This perpetually happy, funny, spontaneous man who never gives up appears utterly defeated. My chest constricts so hard I lose my breath.

His pain becomes my pain.

"We can't give up hope," I say softly, leaning in. This time, I brush my lips against his.

Aaron lets out a stuttering sigh as his eyes slowly close, his hand moving to rest at my waist. "Kiss me again, Clarke."

I scoot in closer, one hand going to his shoulder, the other resting on his chest. The thrum of his heartbeat pulses against my palm, and I dip my mouth to his again.

Aaron's lips part, allowing my tongue to slip easily inside. Something rumbles in his chest, and his fingers contract on my waist. My kiss is medicine to him right now and if this is the only way I can help him—bring some measure of peace to his mind—then I'm all in.

Without hesitation, I swing a leg up and over until I straddle Aaron's lap. His eyes fly open, and the blankness has disappeared. Instead, a flicker of fire lights them. Despite the heaviness of the moment, my body responds to it.

My hands curl into the material of his shirt, and I tip my head to the side. Leaning in, I glide my lips along the strong, corded muscles of his neck. Without hesitation, I drop one hand to the hem of his shirt and snake my hand under it. Running my palm along the ridges of his hard abdomen, I ghost it upward over his chest. Twisting my wrist, I rub a knuckle over one of his nipples. Aaron growls in response. He shifts his body, grips my hips, and presses me down on his pelvis.

The evidence that just the tiniest of touches from me has a big effect—a huge and hard one by the feel of it—goads me into being bolder.

Gives me the courage and power I need to give Aaron pleasure not only when he needs it, but also when I need to give it to him the most.

Scooting backward on his lap, I drop my fingers to the button of his jeans. I do this while looking straight at Aaron, making sure he doesn't need something different from me.

The dark lust swimming in his eyes tells me I'm on the right track.

"I've been thinking of doing this to you for the longest time," I murmur, feeling a bit of heat flush through my cheeks at the admission. "But I've been a little too shy, and, let's face it... you're always in command, Aaron."

His lips curve upward into a soft smile. "You can take command of me any time you want, babe."

"Even if I want to do something like this?" I ask, not intending for my voice to sound all breathy and kitten-like, but it does anyway. The way it makes Aaron's eyes darken seems to indicate he likes it.

My fingers pop his button, and I slowly lower the zipper over the thick bulge. Aaron sucks in a long breath through his nose as I graze my knuckles down the ridge, separated from my skin only by the cotton of his briefs.

I can see a problem right away. Between Aaron's position on the couch, with me on his lap and the fact his enormous erection has made things a bit tight between his briefs and jeans, it's not going to be easy to get at him.

I tip my head up, seeing Aaron as he watches me intently.

Waiting.

In need.

He needs *me*.

I slide off his lap until my knees hit the carpeted floor, Aaron's strong thighs on either side of me. Gently pushing my fingertips into the waistband of his briefs, I say, "Lift your hips for me."

Moving without hesitation, he lifts his butt off the cushion. I tug at the material in my way. First down over one hip, then the other, until I finally ease the material over his hard shaft and release it from its confines.

Over the last few weeks that I've been sexually active with Aaron, I've done my fair share of touching his cock and I've certainly examined it in between kisses and such. But now, I just take a moment to admire the sheer beauty of the part of him that makes him so distinctly male.

He's long and thick, covered in velvet-soft skin, with gorgeous veins running under the dusky color. Aaron keeps himself well-trimmed, and he's like a visual piece of art. I've never given the male anatomy much thought other than for the arousal such an appendage can cause when used correctly, but I swear I could stare at Aaron like this for hours.

Lounging back on my couch, eyes heavy and pants pulled down past his hips, he looks debauched. His thick cock laying heavily against his lower belly, just waiting to be touched.

Or maybe kissed.

Sucked.

I rise up on my knees, bend over Aaron's lap, and run my tongue up the length of him. It's the first time I've touched him there with my mouth. He groans loudly in a mixture of what seems to be pain and pleasure at the same time.

I look up, almost not able to bear what I see in return. His eyes glitter almost dangerously... and the shiver that runs up my spine is delicious.

My hand slides along his thigh, over the bunch of his jeans, and I wrap my fingers around the thick warmth of him. I give a squeeze, bend over his cock once more, and suck the tip of him into my mouth.

"Fuck, Clarke," Aaron growls, his hips jerking upward. I push to take him in even deeper. He's way too large for my mouth to accommodate him fully. When the tip of his cock hits the back of my throat, I fight against my gag reflex.

I may have willingly and foolishly given up my virginity to a man who hadn't deserved it, but this is the first time I've ever had a man in my mouth. And I find this more monumental than anything I could have ever given Tripp. I feel infinitely closer to Aaron while I suck on his length, listening to his moans as I bob up and down while in control of his pleasure.

Aaron's hands come to my head, and for a wild moment, I want to give him control. I want him to grip my head in those large hands of his, then allow him to fuck my throat however he sees fit. Because I trust Aaron to not hurt me—unless it's in a mutual, hurts-so-good way.

But he shows restraint, merely stroking my temples with his thumbs as he steadies my head. I move a hand to the base of his cock, firmly jacking the length of him in the opposite direction of my mouth.

Aaron mutters, alternating between curses and praising me. "Feels so fucking good, Clarke."

With how hard he's breathing and the way his hips are moving under me, I can tell he's getting close.

Suddenly, his hands tighten and he stops my motion. I have him in deep, my tongue flattened on the underside of his enormous shaft, when I look up to find him staring at me with an expression I can't quite gauge.

Awe?

One thumb strokes my cheek as he murmurs, "My cock in your mouth... it's fucking beautiful."

I purr in response, loving how much he's enjoying this. Knocking his hands from my head, I redouble my efforts and start to work his length faster. Aaron groans, curses again, then starts to flex his hips, urging me on.

I stroke him hard, suck him in deep, and squeeze his balls with my other hand. Lust starts to make me dizzy—the realization of my actions turning me on like never before.

And then... Aaron grips me by the nape of my neck, pushing me down firmly on his cock until he's pressing against the back of my throat. I reflexively swallow, feeling the muscles of my throat ripple around him, and he groans out, "Oh, fuck, Clarke... I'm coming."

It's glorious when his hot seed floods my mouth. I swallow over and over again as he releases into me. The feeling that I'm giving him something special— something almost holy between us—overwhelms me. Tears prick at my eyes. It's a feeling I memorize, because I know something monumental has changed between us once again. I now own a piece of him, the way he already owns a part of me.

Aaron gently pulls me off his spent dick, his hands going under my armpits. I feel slightly woozy from my efforts, but I'm satisfied in a way that also has me feeling mellow. Aaron easily lifts me from the floor, pulling me up his body until he settles me on his lap. He shifts so I don't crush his well-used cock, then cuddles me against his chest. Wrapping his arms around me, he presses his face into my neck and murmurs, "You are amazing, Clarke."

Simple words, but the force of emotion behind them hits me in all the feels. I don't feel the need to say anything back, but I do wonder if this is what love feels like...

I wonder if Aaron is thinking along the same lines?

Maybe we'll talk about it soon.

One day.

CHAPTER 23

Wylde

I WALK INTO Baden's room, gritting my teeth at the horror of seeing him in the bed with tubes swirling all around him. He's been heavily medicated since his surgeries, and I still don't understand everything that has happened to him. I've heard everything from lacerated spleen to spinal concussion to brain hemorrhage to… my head spins from it all.

If that isn't bad enough, one of his attackers sliced into his face, cutting him from temple to jaw. There's a jagged line of black stitches running down his face, reminding me of Frankenstein.

Giving him a quick glance, noting he's still sleeping so deeply he doesn't stir, I move past his bed and hand coffees to his parents where they sit on the other side.

"Thanks, Aaron," his mom says with a tired smile. I'd like to say I understand some of their fears right now, but I don't. If I were laying in that bed instead of

Baden, I'm not sure my mom would be by my side.

My dad, well… too late for that, but had he been living… he most certainly would not be here.

I move back to the other side of the room with my own coffee, content to sit and just visit quietly for a few more minutes. We're trying not to overwhelm the Oulett's, but everyone is concerned. When I managed to sneak in about ten minutes ago, I'd immediately volunteered to get them some coffee.

A slight tap on the doorframe has me twisting that way, and I see Dominik. He has a teddy bear in his hand, which seems odd. His gaze locks on Baden's mom, and he glides quietly into the room straight to her.

He hands her the bear, bending to kiss her on the cheek. "Figured you could use something soft to hug once in a while."

To my surprise, she laughs and pats Dominik on the cheek. "That's very sweet."

Dominik shakes Baden's dad's hand before nodding toward the bed. "How is he this morning?"

"He's not woken up yet, but the doctors aren't concerned. They'd rather have him resting. His brain function looks good, though."

"Excellent news," Dominik murmurs, then looks at me. "You good?"

"Good, boss," I reply in a low voice as I push out of

the seat I'd just taken. There are officially too many people in the room now, so I'm going to cede my spot to Dominik. I hold a hand up to his parents. "I'm going to head out to let Dominik visit a bit. You both have my number... call me if you need anything."

"Thanks for coming, Aaron," Baden's dad replies.

I move my gaze to Dominik. "You got a minute before I leave?"

"Sure," he replies easily and follows me out of the room, closing the door behind him.

I move a few doors down, then lean against the wall. Pushing my hands into the front pockets of my jeans, I ask, "What's the latest word on Baden?"

I didn't want to ask his parents, but I know Dominik is being kept in the medical loop since Baden is his player and employee.

Dominik gives a morose shrug. "There's just no telling. Seems like he'll heal fine from the stab wounds while the brain bleed seems to be under control. But the doc said it could go either way on the spinal injury. We just won't know until he's awake and able to undergo some functioning tests."

"Fuck," I mutter, scanning the hallway. "I just can't believe this happened."

"Good reminder that life can change on a dime, right?" he replies.

"Makes you want to grab those you care about and

keep 'em close," I concur.

Dominik claps me on the shoulder and starts to turn back toward Baden's room, but I halt him. "There's actually something else I need to talk to you about."

Pivoting back to me, Dominik cocks an eyebrow at the somber tone of my voice.

"It's personal," I say, setting the tone right off the bat. "Has nothing to do with the organization."

"What can I do for you?" he asks.

Not "What's up?"

But "*What can I do for you?*"

That's just Dominik's way... he's always ready to help one of his guys.

"This may seem like a strange request, but do you have any contacts in Los Angeles who are big in the film industry?"

Dominik jerks his head up, blinking in surprise. "Why? You thinking about going into the movies?"

I laugh, shaking my head. "Not a chance. I'm very happy playing hockey for you."

"Sure," he replies easily. "Frank Cannon is a good buddy of mine."

Now it's my turn to blink. Cannon is only the hottest director in Hollywood right now, and of course, Dominik's good buddies with him. Why wouldn't he be? Dominik is one of the most influential people around right now, as not only the owner of the current

Cup champions built from an expansion draft, but he also owns a championship basketball team and is a multibillionaire.

"Okay... this is going to sound weird," I admit apologetically, "but I could really use his help in getting revenge on someone."

"Excuse me?" Dominik says, his head dipping closer as if he didn't hear me right.

I look left down the hall, then right, noting we're essentially alone. "Okay... going to just lay it out for you. There's an actor out there named Tripp Horschen—"

"The asshole who humiliated your girl," he says bluntly.

"You know about that, huh?" I mutter.

"Willow and I share everything. She told me, and she feels awful for Clarke. But you know I can't support you doing anything criminal, right?"

I glance away for a moment, because, well... technically what I want to do is slightly criminal, but chances of me being caught are slim.

"Okay... here's what I want to do." I take a deep breath, then let it out. I lay my plan out to Dominik, realizing it seems cruel and petty, but it's also a lot better than me going out to Los Angeles to beat the shit out of him.

When I finish, Dominik just shakes his head with a

small smirk. Finally, he says, "I'll call Frank and have him set it up."

"Really?" I ask incredulously. "You don't think this is juvenile and unwarranted?"

Dominik snorts. "If that had happened to Willow, I'd be coming up with something just as devious. Maybe even more so."

"Thanks, Dominik," I say, holding my hand out. He takes it in a side clasp, leans in, and gives me a bro hug.

"Got to look out for my guys," he says with a laugh, clapping my back hard. "Happy hockey players are champion hockey players."

"Agreed," I reply with a grin.

It's funny how I thought I was happy before I met Clarke, but now that she's in my life, I see how lacking it used to be. If I can just get this one thing taken care of—the need to eliminate this burning anger in my gut for what that asshole did to her—then I think it will be the fucking icing on my damn happy cake.

"Are you going to come out to The Sneaky Saguaro tonight?" I ask as we start to walk down the hall together. The exit is back toward Baden's room.

It's one of our rookies, Guy Demere's, turn with the Cup tonight and he has a huge party planned to share his time with all the fans. He chose to have it at The Sneaky Saguaro, which has become the team's official hangout.

"Yeah," Dominik says with a nod. "For a little bit, anyway. I don't want to rain on his parade, despite everything going on here."

As a team, we had thought long and hard about if we should continue going forward with the Cup celebrations that had already been planned out, given the horrific nature of what happened to Baden. It was his father who eventually told us the team had to continue since our victory had been hard-earned. Moreover, he was convinced Baden would want the team to continue the celebrations.

"Clarke and I will see you tonight then," I say. "Although we probably won't stay long."

"Same with Willow and me," Dominik replies. "I'm finding my partying days just aren't as fun as they used to be."

"Word," I agree, giving him a slight punch to the shoulder as we reach Baden's room. I'd much rather stay in with Clarke tonight, but, on the other hand, winning the Cup is a huge freaking deal. It's worth the continual celebrations from the most seasoned player down to the babiest of rookies. Maybe even more so for the rookies.

CHAPTER 24

Clarke

EVEN THOUGH THE atmosphere is incredibly overwhelming, I'm having fun.

For the most part.

I mean, this is my first true taste of Aaron's fame within the hockey world. My first true taste of how devout the Vengeance fan base is.

The Sneaky Saguaro is packed almost shoulder to shoulder, and the vibe is electric. One of the younger players, Guy Demere—whom I'd met at Brooke and Bishop's wedding but had no other conversation with—is the host of this celebratory party. The Cup is set up on the top floor, cordoned off with velvet ropes and bodyguards. Fans, however, have the opportunity to take pictures with it if they're willing to stand in a very long line.

The rest of the players have reserved tables, and we're sort of congregated in an area together. But the fans are free to mix and mingle, so Aaron has been busy with pictures and autographs.

It's what I expected, but I can't say I'm loving having a front-row seat to the female attention focused on Aaron. Sure, I know it's there. I know it will always be there. But Aaron handles everything with grace and ease. If someone gets too handsy, he shuts it down. In all honesty, though, most of the fans are incredibly respectful and are merely excited by his hockey prowess, not looking to get in his pants.

But I know those types are out there, too, which might be why I watch him a little too carefully. Still feeling that doubt within myself, saying how could I be enough for Aaron when he could have any woman he could ever desire.

He desires you, dipshit, I tell myself.

"Penny for your thoughts," a deep voice from my left says. I turn to see Tacker. He'd come alone tonight since Nora's apparently fighting a bad migraine.

I blush deeply, feeling guilt creep up my neck on the off-chance Tacker could actually read my thoughts on my face as I watched Aaron posing for pictures with a group of fans.

"Just wondering how you deal with all this adoration," I quip with a shrug. "Must be exhausting."

Tacker barks out a laugh, placing his forearms on the tall table I'm standing at. Hunkering in a bit closer, because it's quite loud in here, he admits, "To be honest, I hate this shit."

I jerk, whipping my head his way. "You're kidding?"

He shakes his head. "I don't play hockey for this," he replies, sweeping his arm out to indicate the fan fervor. "Well... maybe back in my younger days. I mean, look at Guy over there. See how much fun he's having? This is great for the younger guys."

I glance over at Guy, who is being completely fawned over by a bevy of beautiful women. Aaron had been in that same position many times, I'm sure, and he'd loved it. Why wouldn't he?

"I hope you're not worried about Aaron," Tacker says in a low voice, and my eyes snap back to him. Once again, I flush because the man had to have been reading my thoughts.

"Of course not," I exclaim quickly. Loudly. Almost hysterically.

Chuckling, Tacker puts an arm around me. He gives me a brotherly squeeze, then lets me go. Leaning in a bit closer, he reminds me. "I'm Aaron's best friend. The guy is insanely nuts about you, Clarke. I've never seen him like this."

We both slide our gazes over to him. He has an easy smile on his face as he signs autographs.

"Trust me," Tacker continues as we stare at the man we both clearly care a great deal about. "That man would rather be with you, somewhere alone and quiet, than here right now. But sometimes, we have a duty to our fans that has to be played out."

"I know," I murmur with a sigh. "And I would never hold him back from that."

Tacker nods, accepting my word.

"It's just..." I say, causing his head to turn as he gives me his full attention. "It's still hard to believe sometimes."

"That he's insanely nuts about you?" he inquires.

"That..." I admit with a slight bit of shame that I don't have more confidence. "But all of this, really. It's a bit overwhelming. I never thought I'd be in the middle of such... such..."

"Awesomeness?" he asks with a sly grin.

"I was going to say 'spectacle,' but sure... awesomeness."

We both laugh, and Tacker picks up his beer. He tips it back, draining the last few ounces. When he sets it back down, he nods. "I'm going to head out. I've got a lady with a sore head who needs my attention. But I'd love for you and Aaron to come out to the ranch and hang with us soon, okay?"

"I'd love that," I reply with a smile.

Tacker leans down and hugs me, whispering, "I'm glad Aaron found you."

"Me too," I assure him.

♦

FORTY MINUTES AFTER Tacker leaves, I'm sour again. I suppose it might have to do with more alcohol being imbibed, which apparently makes people bolder.

More assholish.

Aaron does his best to stick by my side when he can, but he's constantly called away by other teammates and fans wanting him to pose for pictures or reminisce over miraculous plays. And, God love him, he's in his element. He's an outgoing and gregarious guy. He may not thrive on the attention, but he is certainly more than comfortable with it.

I fend off drunk men who try to hit on me while Aaron has more than his share of women coming on to him. The only thing that makes it all better is the brief moments of attention he can spare for me, and the way in which he dotes for those few seconds. It might be sweet words or maybe a soft kiss. Regardless, he makes it clear I'm with him and vice versa.

The shame of it is, as the evening progresses, the women seem to care less and less the drunker they get.

Puck bunnies are what I'd heard them called. I think the name is ridiculous.

What's even more ridiculous is how many are super-model gorgeous, tall, and big breasted with very little clothing on. When Aaron poses for pictures, they practically drape themselves over him like fucking curtains.

What's even worse is I get stared at a lot. I'm sure it's just because I'm with Aaron and he's such a star for the team, but it makes me uncomfortable. And maybe I'm being paranoid, but I swear it, too, gets worse as the evening goes on. I even catch people whispering while they stare. Clearly talking about me. I hate every bit of this.

I check my watch for about the hundredth time, not sure what arbitrary number I'm looking for. It's barely eleven o'clock, and the party here at The Sneaky Saguaro is still raging.

Aaron left my line of vision to head to the bathroom, assuring me with a kiss that was way more than a brief peck—it had left me seeing *stars*—that he'd be right back. The other couples we'd hung with in St. John—the women who took me into their group—they've all left and gone home. It's what I want to do as well, and I resolve to ask Aaron if we can leave when he comes back.

I see the top of his head before I can see the rest of him. He winds his way back through the crowd toward me. Some people try to stop him, but he makes quick apologies and sidesteps them. Finally catching my gaze, he mouths a question as he walks toward me. "Ready to go?"

I beam a smile back, nodding my head so vigorously

I'm surprised I don't give myself whiplash.

Aaron returns my grin, and for a moment, we're tightly connected.

And then… his face is blocked, because a tall, beautiful woman with sunny-yellow hair and curves for days in a strapless dress that barely covers her ass steps in front of him. She's wearing platform sandals and her breasts are so big they're practically popping out of the front of her dress.

Her hands go to his chest as she leans in to whisper something in Aaron's ear. My blood pressure spikes, and I feel my ears get hot with anger and shame that this is happening right in front of me.

To Aaron's credit, he shakes his head and tries to step around her.

She moves to cut him off, elegantly holding up a small piece of paper between her first and middle fingers. Boldly, she reaches down and tucks it into his front pocket, whispering something else to him.

I'm so pissed I see red, knowing without a doubt she just tucked her name and number in my boyfriend's pocket.

She just fucking touched him intimately to do it, too.

Aaron's face clouds with anger. Quickly, he moves around her, immediately searching me out. He knows I saw every bit of it.

All I can do is offer him a disappointed look.

Not disappointed *in him*. Just disappointed that we have to put up with crap like this.

Aaron strides past the woman, not sparing her a glance as he approaches me.

"Can we go?" I ask tiredly. "Or if you want to stay, I can Uber it home."

"Of course, we're going," he replies, taking my purse and sliding it on my shoulder. He grabs my hand, then starts leading me down the staircase toward the exit.

People try to stop him, but he blows them off, shoulder turned slightly to push his way through the crowd while pulling me along behind him.

When we get out in the parking lot, Aaron cuts left toward his truck. He offers me an apology. "I'm sorry that happened."

"I can never compete with that," I mutter.

Aaron stops dead in his tracks, then whips around on me. "Why would you think you'd need to?"

I shrug, staring hard at the asphalt parking lot. I'm being lame. I know it.

Aaron's palms are on my face and he forces my gaze up to him. "I don't want that, Clarke."

Staring mutely, I don't say anything.

He tries to shock me. "I've had that. Plenty of it."

I grimace, my gaze cutting off to the side.

"Goddamn it, Clarke," he growls. "I want you. I'm

with you. What the fuck else do I need to do to make you understand that?"

Sighing, I give him a sheepish smile. "I know. This is just new for me. I'll acclimate."

He considers me for a long moment, his eyes boring into mine. I wait for him to say something funny to put me at ease, so we can laugh at my stupidity.

Instead, he just mutters, "I hope so. Because this is my life, and I can't change it."

Then he's tugging me along toward his truck. Opening the door for me as he always does, he helps me climb up into it. When he shuts the door without a word, it stings.

I do believe we've had our first argument. I find I hate it more than I hate watching women fawn all over him.

Resolving to apologize, I get sidetracked when my phone starts ringing.

Veronica's ringtone.

Nabbing my phone as Aaron climbs into the driver's side, I answer before he shuts the door. I can use the diversion for a minute.

"Hey, Veronica," I say purposely, so Aaron knows who's on the phone. He doesn't even glance my way, just starts the engine and reverses out of the spot we're in.

"Hey," she says softly, and I tense at the hesitancy in

her voice. She sounds like she's dreading talking to me, which makes no sense seeing as she's my best friend.

"Is everything okay?" I ask, which gets Aaron's attention. He shoots me a quick look, but I stare out the windshield, feeling trepidation creep up my spine.

"Um… there's something you need to know," she continues gently. "I know you're not on social media…"

When her words trail off, nausea starts to bubble in my gut. Damn right I'm not on social media. I can't stand that shit. Not after I became a viral meme for everyone's sick amusement.

"Tell me," I order. Somehow, I know I must have become a viral story again.

"Um…"

"Just tell me," I yell. Aaron whips his startled gaze my way again as he stomps on the brakes. He jerks the truck into a parking lot, bringing it to a quick stop, but I ignore him.

I clutch hard at the phone as Veronica starts to talk. "Apparently, Aaron posted a picture of you two on Instagram last week. It's a really great picture, actually… looks like a selfie from when you were on the beach."

I remember that. It's the only photo we'd ever taken together selfie-style, and I'd asked him to text it to me. I look at it often because we're both having so much fun and were deliriously happy that day.

"His post outted you as his girlfriend. Very sweet.

And it mentioned your bookstore and the signing."

I slowly swivel Aaron's way. He has parked the truck, and he's watching me worriedly. He has no clue what Veronica is telling me, but he knows I'm starting to get upset.

No wonder so many people came to the bookstore that day, but that doesn't sound so awful.

"But that's not the bad part," Veronica says, and I pinch the bridge of my nose as I feel a massive headache starting.

"What is it?" I mutter, now resigned to the fact I'm going to be in the limelight in a not-so-flattering way again.

"There's a new meme trending on Instagram and Twitter," she says, her sorrow she has to tell me about it clear in her voice. "I'll text it to you. Frankly, it's not that bad, so I don't want you to get upset."

"Text it to me," I order through gritted teeth before hanging up on my best friend.

"What's wrong?" Aaron asks cautiously.

I ignore him, immediately moving to my phone's text icon. A small chime emits, indicating Veronica has sent me the meme.

Swallowing the hard lump in my throat, I tap on the image. Immediately, tears prick at my eyes as I take it in.

It's a split-frame meme. On the left is the picture from the original meme, the still shot of me when Tripp cut me from the show and I have that God-awful look on my face. Next to it is the picture of Aaron and me with big smiles on our faces. Next to the horrid picture of me, there's no doubt we project a level of intimacy.

The caption says, "Hey, Tripp… I've clearly learned a thing or two since our time together."

Blinking back the tears, I subconsciously rub at the burning sensation in my chest. I recognize the sting of shame well.

There's a part of me that can see why Veronica said it's not all that bad. I mean, I'm all happy and fulfilled next to a gorgeous hockey star who puts Tripp to shame.

But the underlying message is painfully humiliating. The caption stating I'd learned a thing or two does nothing but validate the horrible statement I was an awful virginal lay, which went worldwide.

Deep down, I know none of it is true. I realize it shouldn't affect me. I should recognize the good in my life, and I should let this shit go.

But I can't.

I hold my phone out for Aaron to see, then I erupt and let him have it. "Are you happy now? Your social media post has turned me into another meme for people to laugh at."

It's dim in the truck, but I can see Aaron's eyebrows shoot up as he leans toward the phone to see it.

Grimacing, he mutters, "Goddamn it. Fuck."

Jerking the phone back my way, I study it again. A hysterical laugh bubbles out of me, but I snap it off as I stare at the meme. The deluge of emotions hitting me all at once is the most awful thing I've ever experienced in my life. A million times worse than the original meme, because I really didn't have an emotional investment in Tripp.

Not the way I have with Aaron.

It makes the betrayal hurt so much my chest feels like it's going to cave in on itself.

"I'm so sorry, babe," Aaron says, reaching a hand out.

I shrink away from him, tucking my phone against my chest and folding my arms around it. "Can you please take me home?" I ask, my voice cracking from the threat of the full-blown sobs aching to pour out of me.

"Clarke," he murmurs, and the pity in his voice is too much to bear.

"Please," I beg, turning my wrecked face his way. I know the tears that are starting to leak from my eyes will do more for my cause than any words. "Please just take me home."

Misery etches all over his face for the pain he's caused. He merely nods, then puts the truck in gear.

I lean against the passenger door, my head against the glass as he drives me home. The silence is comforting.

I don't bother to change how I know it'll go. When we get there, I let him help me out of the truck. If I'd tried to resist, he'd only insist on it, just like he'll insist on walking me to the door. So, I let him walk by my side while I clutch the phone holding that awful picture to my chest.

When I reach my door, I turn to face him, essentially stopping his progress onto my porch. "I can't do this."

"Can't do what?" he inquires hesitantly, but there's an edge to his tone. He knows exactly what I mean.

"Can't date you. See you anymore. It's too hard for me."

"Because of a silly social media post?" he asks defiantly.

I'm actually stunned he'd make light of it, which fuels my anger. "Silly? It is humiliating. Just like Tripp did—"

"You need to back the fuck up," he snarls, throwing his palm up. "Don't you dare lump me in with that asshole. *Tripp* did something to you—*I did not.*"

"You posted a picture on social media," I accuse.

"So what?" he says. "I posted a pic because I was proud to be with you. I wanted to show my fans who I'd fucking fallen for. It's not my goddamn fault it somehow got turned into something else."

I'm stunned speechless. The power of words fails me at the mention of him falling for me. I mean... what exactly does that *mean*?

I shake my head, the bitter feelings pushing aside any warm emotions or curiosities his declaration tried to build up within me. My pride won't let me explore it.

Because it doesn't matter. At this moment, I can't see past the shame of being a joke to the entire world. Again. This won't be the last time it happens, either.

"I'm not cut out to be in the spotlight like that," I say imploringly... begging him to please understand where I'm coming from. "I thought I could deal with it, but I can't."

"So that's it? You just want to end things?" he asks with a harsh laugh.

Well, shit... the thought of never seeing Aaron again makes me feel like I want to die. "I don't know," I practically wail. "I just know this is the same stuff I went through before. Now, because of you, it's all riled up again, and maybe... maybe I just need some time to think about this."

Aaron takes a step back, and I can tell he's pissed. His sympathy doesn't last long. "You know what? Take all the damn time you want. I'm out of here."

He pivots sharply and bounds down the steps, muttering curses in his wake. He doesn't look back, but angrily hops in his truck and stomps the gas, squealing tires as he leaves.

Dropping to the top step, I stare morosely down the street until his taillights fade away. Realizing I'm still clutching my phone hard in my hand, which is now aching, I pull it away from my chest. The meme glares back harshly.

A surge of anger sweeps through me and I cock my arm back, slamming the phone down onto the concrete sidewalk as hard as I can. It shatters as I expected it to, but at least that horrid meme isn't in my face anymore.

Wrapping my arms around my shins, I put my head on my lap and start to cry.

CHAPTER 25

Wylde

"**D**UDE… YOU ARE practically vibrating," Tacker says, his hand coming down on my shoulder. I glance down at the folder in my hand, gripping it tightly. "You need to take a couple of deep breaths before you go in there," he warns.

In there would be the conference room we're standing outside of in the downtown Los Angeles offices of Frank Cannon. The walls are heavy paneled oak, but there's a vertical pane of glass beside the heavy wooden door and I can see Frank. He sits at a large conference room table with what appears to be a very nervous Tripp Horschen, who repetitively tugs on his tie.

Dominik ended up calling in a huge favor for me, and he'd arranged a telephone call between Frank Cannon and me. I should have felt stupid laying out such a plan, but I didn't. After Clarke essentially broke up with me four days ago, I was more committed than ever on raining retribution down on the man who broke the woman I love, who made it impossible for her to accept me.

To my surprise, Frank thought my plan was brilliant. He's always been known as a bit of a strange duck, but he's so highly respected for his creativity and brilliance it's probably not so surprising he was more than happy to play a role in my revenge plot.

His role wasn't extensive, but it was important. He had his people reach out to Tripp's agent to express interest in casting him in an upcoming Frank Cannon film. Of course, Frank would never do such a thing. His films commanded the most elite Hollywood actors and actresses. Purely A-listers. Tripp couldn't even be considered B-list at this point. My investigator gave me a summary of his less-than-stellar acting career, which included the popular soap opera he was on, which was admittedly a success, but, since then, he's not been able to break into anything big. I knew he'd jump at the chance to have a face-to-face with the undisputed king of directors.

Of course, the guy is an idiot to actually think someone like Frank Cannon would be truly interested in him. If Tripp had an ounce of brains, he might have considered this was a setup.

I'm glad he's stupid because he's waiting in there right now with no clue what he's about to get hit with.

Frank doesn't have a lot of time to spare, so he's only engaging Tripp for a few minutes before he stands from the table. The plan is for him to bring me in for an introduction, then leave to give us privacy so Frank doesn't become an accomplice.

Tripp nods as Frank moves around the table to open the door.

"Good luck," Tacker murmurs, but I don't reply. I'm so thankful he came out to Los Angeles with me to do this. It's been a bro trip, through and through, and he's steadied me greatly. When we arrived yesterday, I just wanted to go to Tripp's house and stomp his ass into the ground. Tacker talked me down, as a best friend should.

Frank gives me a wink when I step into the conference room. I wait until he exits, then close the door behind him.

Brows furrowing in confusion, Tripp half rises from the table, unsure of who I am. I can see he thinks he knows me, but he's not quite sure. Unless he's a super hockey fan, maybe not. If he's been following the rising trend of the new meme with Clarke and me, though, he'll know.

Tripp straightens, deciding to offer me a smile as he buttons his suit jacket. He even sticks his hand out for me to shake, but I ignore it. "I'm Aaron Wylde," I say as I round the corner of the table, moving toward him.

"Does that name ring a bell?"

"Um," he hedges, still not quite sure.

"Surely you know Clarke Webber, right?" My voice is low and dangerous. Recognition flares in his eyes as I come toe to toe with him. I give him a solid push backward, and his knees catch the back of his chair. "Sit down. We need to talk."

Tripp sits, but he immediately holds his hands up. "Look, man… I don't know what you think you're doing interrupting my important meeting with Mr. Cannon."

"This isn't a meeting," I say casually, kicking out the chair beside him and lowering myself into it. "Frank just set this up to get you out here in a neutral territory so we can talk."

Disappointment floods his expression as he realizes I'm on a first-name basis with the great Frank Cannon, while he is not. There will be no Oscar-worthy film role forthcoming for him.

"Clarke Webber," I announce her name again, setting off a small pang in the middle of my chest. The woman who broke my heart because she refuses to be brave enough to work past this with me.

Tripp jolts at my mention of her, and his gaze slides away from me as he mutters, "I didn't make that new meme."

"Ah," I drawl with a wry smile. "You do know who I

am then?"

He nods like a petulant child, still refusing to meet my eyes.

My foot shoots out, kicking him lightly in the shin. "Helps if you give me your attention because what I have to say is important."

"What do you want?" he snaps, finally giving me his regard.

My voice is soft, but penetrating in the silence of the room we're in. "I want you to suffer."

Tripp's eyes grow so large I'm afraid they just might pop out of his head. I find I like the fear on his face. I throw the folder I'd been holding on the table in front him, then nod at it.

He gapes at it like a huge black spider will erupt from the inside if he dares to touch it.

"Open it," I growl.

He jerks and leans forward, gently taking the edge and flipping the folder open. The eight-by-ten glossy photo of him passionately kissing a woman outside of a seedy motel shines like a beacon. Tripp blanches at the irrefutable proof that he's a cheater.

Turns out, the investigator I hired turned up two interesting things about this man. He's a philanderer of the worst sort who routinely cheats on his wife—the woman he proposed to and married on *Celebrity Proposal*—and he desperately needs his wife to survive as she's the breadwinner in the household. After her brush with fame on the reality TV series, she ended up becoming a reporter, then an anchor with one of the national celebrity news stations, while Tripp's career tanked down the toilet.

Closing the folder, Tripp snarls. "So you're going to expose me?"

"Not if you make this right," I say blandly.

Not that he ever could make this right to Clarke. The damage has been done, and the hurt he inflicted on her was too powerful for Clarke to overcome.

Right now, a lot of this is about me and my anger for not only what he did to Clarke, but also for how it has now affected our relationship.

Or lack thereof, as the case may be.

"What do you want?" he asks hesitantly. "A public apology?"

A bark of laughter erupts from me, sounding almost maniacal as I shake my head. Tripp shrinks away from me.

Still chuckling, I say, "No. Clarke would absolutely hate that. She hates attention, unlike you. She'd never want that revived in any way, shape, or form. She's everything you're not and therefore, you couldn't understand the type of damage you inflicted on that beautiful soul, so you could never make it right with her. I'm afraid what I want is going to hurt you a bit."

Tripp's complexion turns a nice shade of green as he swallows hard. "What do I have to do?"

"Simple really." I sit forward in the chair, bracing my elbows on the armrest so I can look him straight in the eye. "You're going to donate $200,000 to a literacy charity that's near and dear to Clarke's heart. You're going to do it anonymously because I don't want you getting any credit for it. Clarke would absolutely hate hearing your name, even though it would be to benefit a great cause she loves. Now, you're going to make that donation and you're going to provide me proof in the form of your bank statement and a receipt from said charity. Oh, and you're not going to claim it on your tax return as a deduction. If you do that, I'll destroy these photos."

"You're fucking crazy," Tripp scoffs, getting a little daring with me now that I've threatened his purse strings. "No way—that's most of my savings."

"Yes, I know." The investigator I paid very good money for was able to illicitly gather Tripp's financial information. The asshole has a little bit more than that in his savings, but not much. "It seems B-rated actors don't make much money in Hollywood, but I have it on good authority you made $200,000 for being on *Celebrity Proposal*. As such, I think that's a sufficient amount to set things right."

Tripp's upper lip curls, his anger and sense of entitlement getting the better of him. "All because of some girl who gave it up?" He sneers. "I didn't make her drop her panties."

In all my years of professional hockey—gliding swiftly on the ice in a breakaway or targeting someone for a hip check—I've never moved as fast as I do now.

I have Tripp pulled up from the chair by the lapels of his jacket, spun, and slammed into the plexiglass window that overlooks the streets of downtown Los Angeles. His head cracks hard against the thickness, and I pull my arm back to deliver a vicious uppercut into his soft belly.

He doubles over, but I haul him up straight again, my fist cocked back for a second strike.

The conference room door flies open and I glance over my shoulder to see Tacker standing there. He had either been watching through the window or felt the shudder from me slamming Tripp into the glass. Either way, he gives me a pointed look and merely shakes his head as if to say, "Don't do it."

Tripp is gagging and wheezing, and I scoff at how pathetic he's acting. With a sigh, I spin him back around and shove him into the chair. Tacker backs out of the room, shutting the door.

I squat beside Tripp's chair, resting my hands on the armrest. He refuses to meet my gaze. "I'm not asking you, Tripp. I'm telling you that you are *going* to do this, or your wife will receive those photos. And then you're going to be out of a marriage, which appears to keep you in a pretty cushy lifestyle from what I can tell. On top of that, Frank Cannon is going to blackball you to the entire industry if you don't make the donation. You won't be able to cut a toilet paper commercial after this."

He still refuses to meet my eyes, but I know he heard my message.

I stand, towering over him. "You're lucky."

That gets his attention, and his head tips back with a hateful glare.

"I could have ruined you in so many ways. I could have just sent that stuff to your wife. I have the connections to blackball you forever. Hell, I could have driven you to homelessness if I wanted to. I'm giving you an easy out by letting you make a difference to people with that donation, and that's going to satisfy my need to beat you to a bloody pulp. Because that's really all I want to do."

"Whatever," Tripp mutters, once again not able to hold my stare. "Are we done?"

I reach into my pocket, then pull out a card with my email on it. Tossing it on the table, I instruct him, "You have two days to get it done. Send me the proof."

Without another word, I whirl away from him and head for the door. Just as I open it, he grumbles, "This is blackmail, you know?"

Glancing back, I give him a bright smile. "Yup. Ain't it grand?"

He flips me off, but he and I both know that donation will get made. He can't afford to go public against me about this, because his wife will find out he's a cheater and his career will be over. It's a risk I know for certain he'll never take, so blackmail is kind of moot.

I step out into the hallway. Tacker leans against the wall, studying me. He finally breaks out into a smile. "Went well, did it?"

"Well, I got to punch him," I reply with a shrug.

We move down the hallway, intent on swinging by Frank's office to thank him for his help. I sort of lied about the blackballing part. I have no clue if Frank would even do that for me, but I'm not about to involve him more than I already have. I just needed a legit place to meet Tripp to offer my deal. The threat of what I could do to the twerp is more than enough.

CHAPTER 26

Clarke

"I T'S CALLED DEPRESSION," Veronica says as I slump on the stool behind the cash register. As a proprietor of a store that depends on customers to come in and buy things so I can make money, I continuously glare at the door and wish for people to stay away.

"I'm not depressed," I mutter.

"On the verge of tears, feels like you're slogging through mud, flat monotone effect. You're depressed."

I swing my gaze from the door to my best friend, who leans on the back counter as she watches me. After Aaron had left the other night and I'd finished crying my eyes out, I'd called Veronica.

She came over, then listened to me recount everything without interruption but for a few well placed "uh-huhs," and "that makes sense," she lent me her rapt attention as only a best friend can do. She didn't offer advice or tell me I was wrong. Of course, she didn't say

Aaron was wrong, either. She merely validated my feelings. It's what I needed then.

Now, four days later, I need someone to just put me out of my misery.

"Let's go through it again," Veronica suggests.

I swivel on the stool, scowling. "I don't want to talk about it anymore. I don't want to think about it. I just want Aaron Wylde and all my memories of him to go away."

"Yeah," she replies dryly. "How's that working for you so far?"

"Shut up," I mutter, swiveling to glare at the door again.

To my shock, it opens and a woman walks through. Tall and gorgeous with dark hair and equally dark eyes set into a modelesque face.

Nora.

I sit up straight with a smile, a concerted move to display false confidence and a general joy for life.

Her keen eyes cut through me as she strolls my way, and I can't help but slump back down. Nora raises an eyebrow at Veronica. "Is she depressed?"

"Yup," she replies.

I whip around to glare at my best friend. "Traitor."

Then I remember my manners, so I make the introductions. "Nora… the woman behind me who thinks I'm depressed even though I'm actually just stoically brooding is my former best friend, Veronica."

"Pleased to meet you," Nora says as she moves around the counter to shake Veronica's hand. "I'm Tacker's wife."

"Aaron's best friend," Veronica exclaims, getting the connection. I've obviously filled her in on everyone she hasn't met yet, but it's a lot of people to keep track of.

Nora puts her purse on the counter, slowly scanning the interior of the store. She walks down the adjacent wall, quietly perusing some of the items for sale. Picking up a ceramic cardinal bird, she flips it over to look at the sticker before setting it down.

Finally, she focuses on me. "You have a lovely place here. Aaron told Tacker and me all about it, and I've been wanting to come see it for myself."

I don't buy that for a moment. Well, I mean yes... I do believe Aaron probably talks about me to his best friend and his wife. I can also believe Nora wanted to come by at some point.

But I don't believe she's just dropping in out of the blue without an ulterior motive.

"Can I help you pick something out?" I offer.

"Actually, no," she replies as she approaches me, coming to stand on the opposite side of the counter. She clasps her hands, placing them on top of the glass case. "I actually came to find out why you so callously cut Aaron out of your life."

My chin jerks inward, and I straighten on my stool.

Veronica murmurs from behind me, "Oh man… this is going to be good."

I don't bother whipping another glare her way. She's already relinquished her title as my best friend.

Nora just appraises me, her spine straight and her stare imperious. A flush of anger that she'd dare to judge my feelings on this matter wells within me, but, just as quickly, I deflate like an old party balloon.

"I'm sorry," I practically moan out the apology, slumping farther down on my stool. I press my forearms to the glass case, dip my forehead to rest there, and rock back and forth. "I don't know what the hell I did or what I'm doing. I messed everything up."

Veronica approaches, soothingly patting my shoulder. "There, there."

I can almost envision her giving a shrug to Nora as if to say, "You brought this out of her. Now what do we do?"

"So fix it," Nora suggests, but her tone is kind and understanding this time.

I lift my head, eyes wide. "But how? I cut him out of my life. I sent him on his way. I wasn't strong enough to stick up for what we had, and he has to think I'm the most pathetic of losers."

Nora rolls her eyes. "Please… you're not giving Aaron enough credit. The man is crazy about you.

Granted, you hurt him, but I'm sure he'll forgive you for it. You just have to reach out."

"Really?" I ask hopefully. Because the reason I am indeed depressed is I thought I'd ruined everything the other night. When I'd told him I couldn't do it, he took me at face value and left without even fighting for me. In my mind, that meant he had moved on.

Nora presses her fingertips to the edge of the case, leaning toward me. "I'm in counselor mode now, okay?"

I nod, eagerly giving her my attention.

"You have insecurities and trust issues. We all do. No sense in denying it or being ashamed of it. It's what makes us human."

I nod again, waiting for that magic kernel of therapeutic advice.

And wait…

Tipping my head slightly, I say, "And…"

"And what?" she scoffs. "Get over it."

"Get over it?" I repeat tentatively, as if testing the weight of this miracle suggestion on my tongue.

"Get over it," she affirms. "You have an amazing man who has accepted you despite your hang-ups and history. He has worked patiently and diligently to make you see him for who he is. He's taken a chance on you, trying something that is foreign to him, while going in full force despite how scared I'm sure he was. And if you can't recognize and understand what an amazing gift that's been handed to you, then you don't deserve him. Back away and let another woman have her chance."

I do not like the sound of that. Don't like one damn thing she just said, even as I recognize the truth in every single word.

"Confront your fears, Clarke," Nora suggests softly. "I promise you, the greatness that awaits on the other side of it is well worth any discomfort you have to face to get there."

"Does he hate me for pushing him away?" I ask, my voice barely registering as I'm so afraid of the answer.

"I don't think Aaron has the capacity to do anything but love you," she replies with a smile.

And just like that, hope springs eternal. Nora's words seemingly make the difference between my pathetic depression that had mired me down into inaction to a new resolution within myself to reach for something with Aaron I believe could be amazing.

Popping off the stool, I look back at Veronica. "I changed my mind. You're my best friend again. Can you watch the store while I go to Aaron's?"

"Sure," she replies brightly, clearly never having accepted my demotion.

"Aaron's not at his place," Nora cuts in.

I spin to face her, an eager pep in my step. "Where is he?"

"Um…" She hesitates slightly before admitting,

"Los Angeles."

I frown. "What's he doing there?"

"He and Tacker went. Boy's trip."

"Boy's trip?" That doesn't seem like something they'd do. "Why?"

"Um…"

"Nora, what are they doing in Los Angeles?"

Her gaze cuts over to Veronica, then back to me. She seems sheepish. "Don't make me reveal it."

I jolt at the realization they're doing something I might not like. There can be no other way to account for her clear unease now that the subject matter has been brought up.

"Is it a secret?" I ask neutrally. "Did Aaron ask you not to tell me?"

"No," she drawls, tipping her head to the side. "But he also had no clue I'd come see you, so it's not like it would be something he would think to tell me to keep quiet. I just know… he probably wouldn't want me to tell you."

"Are they out there seeking women?" I ask, knowing it sounds ridiculous.

Nora actually gasps, slightly outraged. "Of course not."

"Then outside of that, I wouldn't be mad about any reason they went out there."

"Oh, you might be," she mutters.

"Nora," I wail, stretching my arms out in supplication. "Tell me."

I can see the warring struggle in her expression as she considers her loyalty to Aaron, which comes through his best friend and her husband, Tacker, to me... a woman she barely knows.

Ultimately, her loyalty stays with Aaron. Lifting her chin, she says, "It's not my place. You're just going to have to ask him yourself."

I stare mutely, knowing nothing I say will make a difference. She takes my silence as the perfect opportunity to escape. Grabbing her purse, she slings it over her shoulder and exclaims, "I really do have to run. Good talk."

I nod, lost in thought over what Aaron could actually be doing in Los Angeles. The bells tinkle as Nora opens the door and looks back. "Are you mad?"

"Yes," I say truthfully. But not overly so. I just want the truth, but I get why she won't tell me.

"When you're over it, can we go out to lunch sometime?" she asks hesitantly.

"Of course," I reply without any real thought, which proves I can't be all that mad.

She beams a gorgeous smile.

Mine isn't so big, but it is grateful. "Thanks for the advice, Nora. I needed it."

She nods. "Aaron and Tacker are taking the red-eye

back tonight. I have it on good authority Aaron will be—along with the rest of the team—at a Cup party at Jim Steele's house tomorrow night. I'm sure he'd be happy to see you there."

That thought has merit. I could lay in ambush at Aaron's place, but he could still be mad. Maybe not answer the door. It might be better to confront him in a public place.

How's that for a girl who used to shun the limelight, but who will now use it to her advantage?

Nora starts for the door, but turns back once more. "One other thing… just promise me if I'm in your wedding party to Aaron, the dresses won't be hideous."

Laughing, I nod. "I promise."

CHAPTER 27

Wylde

I'LL HAVE TO say, it's refreshing having a hockey party to celebrate the Cup win without having to fend off drunk fans or puck bunnies who don't know how to take "no" for an answer.

Jim Steele's Cup party is more teenager focused, given he has a thirteen-year-old daughter. It seems her entire rising eighth-grade class is here, a mixture of giggly girls and pimply-faced boys sprouting their first chin hairs who are trying to impress them.

It's kind of cute, actually, and again, it's more appealing than an adult party.

Of course, all the players and their significant others are here, so there's plenty of frivolity and drinking. Just in an understated, more private kind of way.

The difference—when contrasting Guy's party at The Sneaky Saguaro and Jim's party here at his house—boils right down to the age differences. Guy is twenty years old. Jim is broaching thirty-three.

Tacker and Nora make their way over to where I stand in the corner of Jim's living room. He and his wife separated a few months ago—just as the playoffs were gearing up. I don't pretend to know anything about the cause, but Jim has been struggling to find his footing as a single dad sharing custody of his daughter, Lucy, with his estranged wife.

Tacker hands me a beer.

"Thanks," I reply, noting Nora's not drinking anything. I tease her, saying, "You the DD tonight?"

"Um…" she hems, her face flushing as she looks to Tacker in a panic.

Tacker just stares at her.

"What's going on?" I ask, thinking their vibes are very weird tonight.

Then it hits me… Nora's not drinking. Not that she's a big drinker, but she'll usually have a beer when we're all out like this.

"Holy shit," I drawl. "You're…"

"Not announcing it to the world," Tacker growls in a low voice, cutting me off.

"Pregnant?" I whisper.

Nora steps in closer, her eyes bright with excitement. "We just took the test this morning. I mean… we can't be any more than six weeks, so we're not saying anything to anyone yet."

I make a mock motion of zipping my lips, then throw the pretend key over my shoulder. "Scout's honor. But would it be weird if I hugged you right now? Would that give it away?"

Nora smirks. "Yes. People would find that incredibly odd."

"Fist bump then," I exclaim, holding my fist out to her. When she taps hers against mine, I spread my hand, wiggling my fingers and murmuring. "Blow it up."

Tacker snorts, muttering. "You two are beyond weird."

I can't fucking contain myself. Putting my arm around Tacker's shoulders, I pull him in for a tight side-hug—people thinking it's weird be damned. "I'm so fucking happy for you, dude. I'm going to be an uncle."

"More like a godfather," Tacker replies.

"Really?" I exclaim, my eyes going wide. "That's a huge responsibility. I'm here to tell you that I'm ready for it."

Tacker mutters something like, "Shut the fuck up," but I'm distracted by the buzz of my phone. Ever since Clarke gave me the brush-off five days ago, I've been hawking my messages in the vain hope she'll reach out.

So far, I've been disappointed each time.

My notification is for an email. When I tap on the icon, I'm jolted with a surprise I sort of expected, but it's still slightly shocking when I see it.

An email from Tripp Horschen.

His message is short and simple, but it gives me exactly what I asked for.

> Attached is a copy of my bank statement and the receipt from the literacy charity showing my donation.
> Now fuck off.

Chuckling, I tap on the JPG images, feeling some of the weight slide off my shoulders at the clear evidence this asshole is $200,000 poorer while a good charity's coffers have risen.

Turning my phone toward Tacker and Nora, I tell them, "Tripp came through. Donation has been made."

Tacker taps his beer bottle against mine, and we all take a moment to soak in the fact I successfully blackmailed that asshole as a means of punishment to salve my anger. I'm probably going to hell for this, and yet... I don't feel bad in the slightest.

I start to tuck my phone back in my pocket when it buzzes again.

This time, I have a text and as I glance at it, a bolt of what feels like lightning rockets through my body as I realize it's from Clarke.

Two simple words. *I'm sorry.*

She could have given me a million words—I would have accepted any—yet she offered the two that made everything right in my world in one fell swoop. Here I had been convinced we were irrevocably over with, yet she has opened the door to a future with that apology.

Still, I can't help but play a little hard to get. *For what?*

Before she can reply, I give Tacker and Nora an apologetic smile. "I'll be back."

Moving through the crowd, I make my way from the living room, through the kitchen, and into a mudroom that is thankfully quiet and without people. I lean against the wall, waiting for her reply.

It doesn't come soon enough, but when it does, it has me laughing.

For being stupid.

God, she's adorable. And while I really want to ask if she's at her house so I can rush over to see her, I continue the little game.

How so?

Her reply is simple, but manages to boil down to simplest terms everything that went wrong.

For blaming you for something you had no control over.

If she were here right now, I'd take her in my arms and say I understand her fears and I'm just glad she's talking to me again. As long as we're talking, we can fix anything.

But I want just a little more from her. She put me through hell these last few days, and I want to know if she really has moved past her hang-ups.

So I press her for more revelations by texting back.

And...

There's no immediate response. I wonder if I pushed a little too hard to get her to continue talking out her feelings. If there's one thing I've learned about Clarke, it's that she sometimes needs to take things in baby steps.

I startle when there's a tap on my shoulder. Turning in irritation to see who would be bothering me when I'm in the middle of something so important, I freeze when I'm met by my very own beautiful but frustrating girl staring from behind her glasses. She shrugs, giving me a sheepish grin, and answers my last text. "For waiting this long to apologize. I should have driven after you the night you left my house."

I shove my phone in my pocket, take her by the shoulders, and jerk her to me. Dipping down, I rub my nose along her cheek and murmur. "I'm just glad you came to your senses."

Clarke throws her arms around my shoulders, hugging me tightly. "I'm really sorry, Aaron. I was awful to blame you, especially because you are the most amazing person I've ever known, and I know, deep in my soul, you'd never do anything to hurt me."

"It's okay," I reassure her, burying my face in her neck.

"I love you," she says, her words clear and true. My head pops up so I can see her face, and there's nothing but conviction in her expression. We've never talked about the depth of past relationships, but I can tell this is the first time she's ever said those words to a man.

Just as this is the first time I'll give them to a woman. "I love you, too, Clarke. So much."

There's a kiss that follows our proclamation. As usual, we both get lost in it. I find myself sinking into it, willing to stay gone in this moment forever, but Clarke apparently has other things that still need to be discussed.

She pulls her mouth from mine, giving me a slight push backward. "Now… want to tell me why you were in Los Angeles?"

I hesitate way too long before I drawl, "Um… not really."

Clarke merely cocks a beautifully arched auburn brow, and I know I'll never be able to keep this secret from her.

With a sigh, I admit, "I went to see Tripp Horschen."

She doesn't even react, which tells me she'd already pretty much guessed. "And is he alive?"

"He might have a sore gut," I admit, this time not able to hide the satisfied smirk that comes to my face. "And his bank account might be lighter."

"You stole money from him?" Clarke gasps, her hand flying to her mouth.

I roll my eyes. "Of course not. I merely convinced him to donate to your favorite literacy charity in the amount of $200,000, which is the amount he was paid to be on that stupid fucking show."

Clarke's eyes narrow slightly, but I can't tell if I've offended her or not. On one hand, I know she would rather just let all this die down and never think about it again. On the other, I was merely seeking justice, which, it has to be said, is a noble endeavor.

It appears she's impressed and touched by my efforts since she throws herself into my arms, hugging me tightly as she proclaims, "You're my hero."

Fuck... that makes me feel as good as hearing she loves me.

You think we'd stay in that moment forever, relishing the fact we've come back together and we've acknowledged there's real love between us and we have a future filled with so much promise.

But no.... women have to go and ruin everything.

"Clarke? I didn't know you were here."

I recognize Blue's voice behind us. Clarke pulls away from me, and I want to snatch her back. Before I can even glare at Blue or snarl with propriety, Pepper appears and literally yanks Clarke out of the mudroom. "I'm so glad you're here. We're getting the group together for a picture with the Cup."

I look past Pepper to see Brooke, Regan, Willow,

and Nora.

"Come on," Pepper says, tugging Clarke by the hand away from me. I start to follow, but a hand comes out, tagging me in the chest and pushing me back.

It's Tacker.

He merely shakes his head with a wry smile, "It's a women's picture, dude. Us men aren't invited."

I want to be offended, but as I watch Clarke following the girls with a huge smile on her face, I can't be offended. The message is clear. She's part of the family now.

"Did you tell her what you did with Tripp?" Tacker asks.

"Not the sordid details, but enough to know I'm going to get very lucky later tonight."

Tacker snorts, clapping me on the shoulder. "You know… this has been quite the summer of weddings."

"Four so far," I reply with a nod, watching Clarke as she heads through the kitchen into the living room as the women all move around the Cup.

"You could make it five," he says with a sly smile. "An elopement would be cool."

While the thought of marriage settles on me like a warm blanket, I do know it's way too soon for that. Clarke's also the type who deserves all the romance of an over-the-top proposal and a huge wedding if she so desires. I'm not going to take that from her.

What I am going to do, though, is make sure she knows how much I love and cherish her. Every single day.

Her gaze moves through the crowd, and we lock eyes. Everyone else disappears for just a second as a silent acknowledgment passes between us that tonight is the beginning of forever.

She smiles, loops her arms around her new female Vengeance family, then strikes a goofy pose for the camera.

Fuck, but I love her.

Get your next Sawyer Bennett read for FREE!! Meet the team at Jameson Force Security with a **free download** of *Code Name: Genesis*, a second chance, romantic suspense standalone. Get your copy here: https://dl.bookfunnel.com/xi7ulj9f48

The Arizona Vengeance series continues with *Kane,* a standalone friends-to-lovers hockey romance releasing September 15, 2020! Preorder *Kane* and see all of the books in the Arizona Vengeance series here: sawyerbennett.com/bookstore/the-arizona-vengeance-series

Go here to see other works by Sawyer Bennett: https://sawyerbennett.com/bookshop

Don't miss another new release by Sawyer Bennett!!! Sign up for her newsletter and keep up to date on new releases, giveaways, book reviews and so much more. https://sawyerbennett.com/signup

Connect with Sawyer online:

Website: sawyerbennett.com

Twitter: twitter.com/bennettbooks

Facebook: facebook.com/bennettbooks

Instagram: instagram.com/sawyerbennett123

Book+Main Bites:

bookandmainbites.com/sawyerbennett

Goodreads: goodreads.com/Sawyer_Bennett

Amazon: amazon.com/author/sawyerbennett

BookBub: bookbub.com/authors/sawyer-bennett

About the Author

Since the release of her debut contemporary romance novel, Off Sides, in January 2013, Sawyer Bennett has released multiple books, many of which have appeared on the New York Times, USA Today and Wall Street Journal bestseller lists.

A reformed trial lawyer from North Carolina, Sawyer uses real life experience to create relatable, sexy stories that appeal to a wide array of readers. From new adult to erotic contemporary romance, Sawyer writes something for just about everyone.

Sawyer likes her Bloody Marys strong, her martinis dirty, and her heroes a combination of the two. When not bringing fictional romance to life, Sawyer is a chauffeur, stylist, chef, maid, and personal assistant to a very active daughter, as well as full-time servant to her adorably naughty dogs. She believes in the good of others, and that a bad day can be cured with a great work-out, cake, or even better, both.

Sawyer also writes general and women's fiction under the pen name S. Bennett and sweet romance under the name Juliette Poe.

CPSIA information can be obtained
at www.ICGtesting.com
Printed in the USA
LVHW011609170920
666362LV00013B/1323